LITERATURE FROM CRESCENT MOON PUBLISHING

The Ecstasies of John Cowper Powys
by A.P. Seabright

Postmodern Powys: New Essays on John Cowper Powys
by Joe Boulter

Thomas Hardy and John Cowper Powys: Wessex Revisited
by Jeremy Mark Robinson

Sexing Hardy: Thomas Hardy and Feminism
by Margaret Elvy

Thomas Hardy's Jude the Obscure: A Critical Study
by Margaret Elvy

Thomas Hardy's Tess of the d'Urbervilles: A Critical Study
by Margaret Elvy

Thomas Hardy: The Tragic Novels
by Tom Spenser

Stepping Forward: Essays, Lectures and Interviews
by Wolfgang Iser

Lawrence Durrell: Between Love and Death, Between East and West
by Jeremy Mark Robinson

Andrea Dworkin
by Jeremy Mark Robinson

German Romantic Poetry: Goethe, Novalis, Heine, Hölderlin, Schlegel, Schiller
by Carol Appleby

Rilke: Space, Essence and Angels in the Poetry of Rainer Maria Rilke
by B.D. Barnacle

Rimbaud: Arthur Rimbaud and the Magic of Poetry
by Jeremy Mark Robinson

Shakespeare: Love, Poetry and Magic in Shakespeare's Sonnets and Plays
by B.D. Barnacle

Cavafy: Anatomy of a Soul
by Matt Crispin

Feminism and Shakespeare
by B.D. Barnacle

The Poetry of Landscape in Thomas Hardy
by Jeremy Mark Robinson

D.H. Lawrence: Infinite Sensual Violence
by M.K. Pace

D.H. Lawrence: Symbolic Landscapes
by Jane Foster

The Passion of D.H. Lawrence
by Jeremy Mark Robinson

Samuel Beckett Goes Into the Silence
by Jeremy Mark Robinson

In the Dim Void: Samuel Beckett's Late Trilogy: Company, Ill Seen, Ill Said and Worstward Ho
by Gregory Johns

Andre Gide: Fiction and Fervour in the Novels
by Jeremy Mark Robinson

Julia Kristeva: Art, Love, Melancholy, Philosophy, Semiotics
by Kelly Ives

Luce Irigaray: Lips, Kissing, and the Politics of Sexual Difference
by Kelly Ives

Hélène Cixous I Love You: The Jouissance of Writing
by Kelly Ives

Emily Dickinson: *Selected Poems*
selected and introduced by Miriam Chalk

Petrarch, Dante and the Troubadours: The Religion of Love and Poetry
by Cassidy Hughes

Dante: *Selections From the Vita Nuova*
translated by Thomas Okey

Friedrich Hölderlin: *Selected Poems*
translated by Michael Hamburger

Rainer Maria Rilke: *Selected Poems*
translated by Michael Hamburger

RETHINKING POWYS

RETHINKING POWYS

Critical Essays On John Cowper Powys

Edited by Jeremy Mark Robinson

CRESCENT MOON

Crescent Moon Publishing
P.O. Box 393
Maidstone
Kent
ME14 5XU, U.K.

First published 1999. Second edition 2008.
© The contributors 1999, 2008.

Printed and bound in Great Britain
Set in Rotis Serif 9 on 13pt.
This book is part of the John Cowper Powys Studies Series.

The right of Jeremy Robinson to be identified as the editor of this book has been asserted generally in accordance with sections 77 and 78 of the Copyright, Designs and Patents Act 1988

All rights reserved. No part of this book may be reprinted or reproduced, stored in a retrieval system, or transmitted, in any form or by any means, electronic, mechanical, photocopying, recording or otherwise, without permission from the publisher.

British Library Cataloguing in Publication data

Rethinking Powys: critical essays on John Cowper Powys. -
(John Cowper Powys Studies Series)
1. Powys, John Cowper, 1872-1963 - Criticism and interpretation
I. Robinson, Jeremy
823.9'12

ISBN 1-86171-167-0
ISBN-13 1861711670

Contents

Note on Contributors   *11*

Jeremy Robinson	Introduction: Rethinking John Cowper Powys	*15*
Janina Nordius	*Wolf Solent*: Towards a Discourse of Solitude	*27*
H.W. Fawkner	Venus: Phenomenology of the Beginning of Movement in *A Glastonbury Romance*	*47*
Ian Hughes	The Genre of John Cowper Powys's Major Novels	*73*
Joe Boulter	*The Inmates*, Deleuze/ Guattari, Foucault, and Madness	*91*

Note on contributors

Joe Boulter is Senior Scholar at Somerville College, Oxford. He completed his D.Phil. on John Cowper Powys in 1998. A book of essays, Postmodern Powys) is published by Crescent Moon.

Harald Fawkner is Professor of English Literature at Stockholm University. His books include *The Ecstatic World of John Cowper Powys* (1986) and *Amorous Life: John Cowper Powys and the Manifestation of Affectivity* (Crescent Moon, 1998). He has also published on Shakespeare (1992), John Fowles (1984), and Charles Dickens (1977).

Ian Hughes is lecturer in English at Normal College, Bangor, Wales. He edited the 1990 edition of Powys's *Maiden Castle*.

Janina Nordius is a lecturer in English at Gothenburg University, where she wrote her PhD thesis on John Cowper Powys (this was published in 1997 as *"I Am Myself Alone": Solitude and Transcendence in John Cowper Powys*).

Jeremy Robinson's books include *Glorification: Religious Abstraction in Renaissance and 20th Century Art* (1990), *Arthur Rimbaud* (1992), *Lawrence Durrell* (1995), *The Sacred Cinema of Andrei Tarkovsky* (2006) and *J.R.R. Tolkien* (2008).

JEREMY ROBINSON

Introduction: Rethinking John Cowper Powys

John Cowper Powys (1872-1963) was part of a large, talented family (Theodore, John Cowper and Llewelyn being the most prominent in the literary world). By the time he started writing his most admired works around 1929 – the four Wessex novels (*Wolf Solent, A Glastonbury Romance, Weymouth Sands* and *Maiden Castle*), the two Welsh epics (*Owen Glendower* and *Porius*), and the unsurpassed *Autobiography* – Powys was in his late fifties, and had already been a philosopher, a successful lecturer, a storyteller, a would-be magician and a poet. Powys loved writing, whether it was letters, essays, novels or philosophical commentaries. He lived mainly from his writing after 1930, after nearly 30 years of lecturing (mainly in the United States). He produced many books, which included novels, philosophical essays, poetry, correspondence and literary criticism. Some of the writers that Powys knew personally included Theodore Powys, Llewelyn Powys, Louis Wilkinson, Theodore Dreiser, Thomas Hardy, William Barnes, W.B. Yeats, Dorothy Richardson, Aleister Crowley and Bertrand Russell. In America, Powys was friends with Dreiser, Edna Vincent Millay, Edgar Lee Masters, and Arthur Davison Ficke. He also met E.E. Cummings, Amy Lowell, Edmund Wilson, F. Scott Fitzgerald, Marianne Moore, Ford Maddox Ford and Will Durant, and performers such as Charlie Chaplin and Isadora Duncan.

A mainstream publisher in Britain is yet to take up John Cowper Powys's major works and make them widely available.1 Until that happens, Powys will remain a marginal presence in literature. But John Cowper Powys is as important, significant, great (however one wishes to describe it) as any of the lauded modernists, such as James Joyce, T.S. Eliot, Ernest Hemingway, Marcel Proust and André Gide. On the critical side, Powys criticism is also suffering. It is mainly confined to small presses or the smaller university presses. Gone are the days, it seems, when literary criticism of John Cowper Powys was published by a mainstream house (Methuen publishing G. Wilson Knight's *Saturnian Quest* or Oxford University Press publishing Glen Cavaliero's *John Cowper Powys,* for example). It's important that evaluation of Powys appears outside of a few localized publications. The lack of an easily applicable literary frame-of-reference for Powys's fiction has surely contributed to his neglect by many critics. In appreciating Powys's fiction one has to apply William Wordsworth's famous dictum in the *Lyrical Ballads* that 'every great and original writer... must himself create the taste by which he is to be relished' (*Preface*). Every writer creates their own world, but Powys's fictive world stands apart from those of his contemporaries. He is an original – a British oddity, a one-off like Lewis Carroll, Sir Thomas Browne, Mervyn Peake, Robert Graves and D.H. Lawrence. G. Wilson Knight called Powys 'perhaps the greatest of all novelists'.[2] H.W. Fawkner suggested that John Cowper Powys is 'a man of letters without really existing in literature'; he is a potentially disruptive force in literature, and probably enjoys such disruptions.[3] Fawkner says that Powys cannot be judged by the usual mechanisms of literary criticism (ib., 178). This is one reason for Powys's continuing lack of recognition amongst literary critics. Putting it simply, the usual mechanisms of traditional (humanist) criticism do not work with John Cowper Powys. His fiction is a slippery presence, refusing to be nailed down to any particular interpretation, or to be put into the standard literary categories. Powys's fiction seems to be in an 'elsewhere', a place which traditional literary criticism cannot circumscribe. It is ungraspable but not ineffable, mystical but not beyond reach. Poet Penelope Shuttle suggested, persuasively I think, that Powys is such a huge presence in literature he becomes invisible. 'He is like a mountain so huge and high that paradoxically he becomes invisible to the literary world'.[4] He is the ghost of modernism, present but unacknowledged, the literary giant that no one can see (or is willing to see). Powys's fiction deals with things that cannot be seen or easily spatialized or quantified – affectivity (or feelings), in Fawkner's terms.

One senses frustration with traditional criticism's treatment of Powys's fiction: what is it about? What is it? What are its pleasures, its successes, its failures? One detects that Powys's fiction is (or would be) difficult to market on a mass scale, a problem for the contemporary publicity department or slick, urban advertizing agency. Take one of the three key Powys works, *Wolf Solent* (*Autobiography* and *A Glastonbury Romance* probably being the other two): what is *Wolf Solent* about? How would it be marketed to booksellers and consumers? The 1982 Penguin Modern Classics edition of *Wolf Solent* was described on the back cover as 'one of the few great apocalyptic novels of our time... Complex, humorous, romantic and sometimes extravagant'. The publisher's blurb described *Wolf Solent* as 'the story of a young man returning, after ten years in London, to work as a literary assistant near the school where his own father had been History Master'. Plot or story is one way PR departments sell products (notably Hollywood movies). News on TV and radio is also couched as narratives. However, the narrative strategies of Powys's fiction are quite different from conventional fiction. Selling *Wolf Solent* on its plot alone would miss the point and substance of the book. Powys's narrator employs the plot device of Wolf returning to his West Country homeland as a rather tired and ancient method of introducing the reader to the main character and the setting. However, such conventional plot mechanisms are soon dropped in favour of Powys's explorations of sensuality, nature, place, memory, childhood, ancestral history, sexuality, spirituality and personal relationships. *Weymouth Sands* was marketed by Picador/ Macmillan (in the 1980 paperback) as a book in which Powys 'created a wealth of characters and showed his deep sympathy for the variety, the eccentricity, the essential loneliness of human beings'. At least that publisher's blurb noted the fundamental unconnectedness of the characters in *Weymouth Sands*. The 1975 Picador paperback publicity of *A Glastonbury Romance* emphasized the mystical, mythic aspects of the novel. The quotes from Colin Wilson and Russell Hoban spoke of the mystical achievements of *A Glastonbury Romance*: 'the Tolkien generation's next adult novelist', Hoban was quoted as saying. This fitted in with the post-hippy era mid-1970s. The cover for the 1975 edition was distinctly, luridly psychedelic. 'An epic novel that recreates the eternal legend of the Grail' said the blurb. But selling *A Glastonbury Romance* as a worthy successor to *The Lord of the Rings* is bound to fail, because Powys's project moves far beyond Tolkien's Middle Earth yarns with their dualistic, Christian outlook and conservative, royalist, pro-militaristic ideology. What Powys does *not* write is would-be 'epic' fantasy or science fiction books. *A Glastonbury Romance* is very definitely *not* part of that sub-genre of fantasy fiction dealing with Arthurian and sword and sorcery themes (authors of this kind of fiction include Stephan Lawhead and Nikolai Tolstoy).

The main Powys critics include G. Wilson Knight, John Brebner, Glen Cavaliero, H.P. Collins, Morine Krisdóttir, Charles Lock, Richard Maxwell, C.A. Coates, H.W. Fawkner, R.P. Graves, Kenneth Hopkins, Roland Mathias, Jeremy Hooker, Belinda Humfrey, W.J. Keith, Janina Nordius, Michael Ballin, Oliver Wilkinson, Denis Lane, Derek Langridge, Louis Wilkinson and Colin Wilson. There have also been a number of important admirers of Powys who have not written as much as some of the main Powys critics, but who have helped to promote him in the world of literature: P.J. Kavanagh, Penelope Shuttle, Angus Wilson and George Steiner. Powys can be approached from so many different positions that each critic 'is driven to make his own little world, his own enclave or mode of insight'.[5] Powys critics often disagree about the meaning of Powys's writing, and how he should be interpreted and discussed. Some critics, such as G. Wilson Knight and H.W. Fawkner, are regarded as inspiring but somewhat eccentric, indulged but not taken too seriously. However, no critic's writing on John Cowper Powys has exceeded the strangeness of Powys's works. It is often the more unusual approaches to Powys's work, such as by Fawkner or Knight, that are more illuminating than the conventional critics. But even the more traditional, humanist approaches to Powys's *œuvre* (such as by H.P. Collins, Glen Cavaliero, John Brebner, Kenneth Hopkins and Denis Lane) sometimes contain distinctly odd, idiosyncratic views. Powys is the kind of writer that encourages a huge variety of critical interpretations (though not as many, yet, as Shakespeare or James Joyce). One only has to compare the many essays on, say, *Wolf Solent* or *Porius*, to see how the approaches to Powys's writing differ and conflict. Some critics have suggested that it is precisely the lack of a single, dominant interpretation of Powys's works which is 'the most life-giving aspect of his books' (ib., 134). Powys has not been colonized by any single critic nor any particular critical approach (like F.R, Leavis with D.H. Lawrence). His works are still open, up for grabs. Like any author, Powys's works can be appropriated by any theory or ideology, such as Marxism, materialism, feminism, deconstruction and psychoanalysis. Powys's works could be approached from the vantage point of Julia Kristeva's *chora* or Kristevan abject, or Wolfgang Iser's reader-reception theory, or Jacques Derrida's deconstruction, or Jean Baudrillard's theory of 'simulations', or Fredric Jameson's 'hyperspace', or Terry Eagleton's Marxist literary criticism, or Roland Barthes' 'death of the author', or Jonathan Dolimore's cultural materialism, or Teresa de Lauretis's feminist critique of cinema, or Edward Said's Orientalism, or Gayatri Chakravorty Spivak's postcolonial theory, or Monique Wittig's lesbian otherness, or Jean-Paul Sartre's existentialism, or Elizabeth Grosz's philosophy of the body, or Stephen Greenblatt's New Historicism, or Laura Mulvey's theory of the female gaze, or Hélène Cixous' *jouissance* of writing, or Elaine Showalter's wild zone'. One could imagine essays on the Kristevan abject in Powys's use of vivisection in *Weymouth Sands*. Or the disappearance of subjectivity and self in Powys's works in the light of the 'hyperreal' philosophies of Jean Baudrillard and Umberto Eco. Or the postmodernism of *Porius, à la* Fredric Jameson and Jean-François Lyotard. It could be very exciting having a major critic such as Elizabeth Grosz, Stephen Heath, Eve Kosofsky Sedgwick, Kaja Silverman or Alice Jardine taking on Powys. While one imagines that thinkers such as Catherine Belsey, Harold Bloom, Alan Sinfield, Wolfgang Iser and J. Hills Miller would contribute much to Powys studies, some Powys admirers might be wary of certain critics approaching Powys's work: the simplistic second wave feminism of Kate Millett, for example, whose *Sexual Politics* churned up D.H. Lawrence and one of Powys's long-time correspondents, Henry Miller, in a disastrous but influential mis-reading; or the left-leaning, (post-) Marxist thinkers (such as Louis Althusser, Raymond Williams, Georg Lukács, Stuart Hall, Terry Eagleton, Walter Benjamin and Mikhail Bakhtin). Those who cherish Powys might recoil from him being appropriated by the stranger, denser, more 'difficult' and eccentric contemporary theorists (such as Jean Baudrillard, Jacques Derrida, Monique Wittig or Guy Debord). And if the critics whose specialities include lesbian, queer and S/M issues (such as Sheila Jeffreys, Judith Butler, Rosi Braidotti, Teresa de Lauretis, Karla Jay, Stevi Jackson or Bonnie Zimmerman), got hold of Powys's work, bafflement might ensue. (Recall, though, that Powys included gay and lesbian characters in his fiction, as well as a host of more unusual sexual practices). However, it is worth remembering that the works of writers such as James Joyce, Joseph Conrad, Thomas Hardy and D.H. Lawrence, contemporaries of Powys, have been given the postmodern/ cultural theory treatment and have been enriched by it. And whatever Joyce, Conrad, Hardy and Lawrence can endure critically, so can Powys. (Joyce, like Samuel Beckett, has attracted some of the most important cultural critics, such as Derrida, Cixous, Jameson, Williams, Heath and Iser).

A standard movement in criticism exalts postmodernism via modernism. The 'classic' modernists are exalted by the 'classic' postmodernists: Flaubert, Balzac and Brecht by Barthes; Proust by Deleuze/ Guattari; Proust and Rilke by de Man; Conrad by Edward Said; Magritte by Foucault; Artaud, Joyce, Lautréamont, Céline and Mallarmé by Kristeva; Mallarmé, Joyce and Artaud by Derrida; Proust by Gérard Genette; Balzac, Conrad and Gissing in Jameson; Sterne by Lyotard; Pater and Sterne by Iser; Hardy, Dickens, James and Trollope by Hills Miller; Genet, Kafka, Rimbaud, Kleist, Hölderlin and Proust by Cixous.[6] Just as the same authors keep recurring in the work of contemporary theorists, so do the same philosophers: Nietzsche, Freud, Marx, Saussure, Hegel, Husserl, Sartre, Althusser, Wittgenstein, Benjamin and Bakhtin.

In the essays in this book, Janina Nordius cites Nietzsche and William James; H.W. Fawkner uses Arthur Schopenhauer and Michel Henry; Ian Hughes cites Walter Pater, Sir Thomas Browne and C.G. Jung; Joe Boulter refers to Gilles Deleuze and Félix Guattari, Michel Foucault, Wilhelm Reich and Thomas Pynchon.

Many of the writers contemporary theorists cite are the tried and trusted big names of the literary world. Writers such as Shakespeare, Joyce and Dante, for example, have vast scholarly universes built up around them, which are being expanded all the time, unlike Powys. Every year hosts of new articles, monographs, reviews and deluxe collector's edition clothbound books are published on Dante, Joyce, Shakespeare, Rimbaud and Dostoievsky, while on Powys there is very little.

John Cowper Powys's writings refuse to be locked into a single category or reading; sometimes mystical, they can also be intentionally bathetic; if sincere and serious, they can also be comic and disruptive; solemnity is sustained for pages, but irony and playfulness are never far away. 'If he turns out to be a mystic, he will be a peculiarly restless one for cluttered and modern times'.[7]

H.W. Fawkner suggested that the 'mundane approach to the works of Powys' was 'anthropocentric, anthropological, psychological, biocentric, biological, biographic.'[8] The non-mundane outlook (which was Fawkner's) was 'phenomenological, mystical'. Approaching Powys's works from a mundane angle meant neglecting 'the life-intimacy that antecedes mind and world' wrote Fawkner (ib., 29). 'Powys's life-achievement is an attack on this mundanizing of life' and critics who treated Powys as mere ego, mind, psychology or creature weakened Powys's attack, 'turning the dedication of a writer's life into a joke' (ibid.).

John Bayley suggested that Powys had not become popular partly because he did not offer an amenable world to readers, that was reassuring and exact. Unlike Graham Greene, said Bayley, Powys was 'happily and magnificently deficient' in imposing his world on the reader.[9] For Bayley, Powys did not present worlds which the reader could enter; nor did he employ symbols, as many writers do. I think Powys did try to create worlds. He certainly spoke of living inside certain realms when he wrote his novels. Powys's letters show how much he lived in 499 AD when he was writing *Porius*, for example. Although Powys's worlds are not the same as those of Thomas Hardy or J.R.R. Tolkein, they are carefully constructed spaces, in which the reader can wander if they wish. If Powys did not create amenable worlds, as Bayley suggested, his fiction would not have the force that it does. The same goes for characters: although Powys's characters are quite different from those of conventional fiction, they must still retain elements of credibility for the fiction to work at all. There must be some correlative between Powys's characters and 'real', flesh-and-blood people, as the reader knows them, for the fiction to work. For Walter Allen, even though Powys might have been a genius, one can be 'thoroughly dissatisfied with what he has made of it'. Powys's creation of a world of elemental and natural forces makes his work 'so alien to the temper of the age as to be impossible for many people to take seriously' said Allen in *Tradition and Dream*.[10]

There was yet another resurgence of interest in Powys in 1998: Chris Woodhead, the government's Chief Inspector of Schools, mentioned the Powys brothers in a review of *The New Oxford Book of English Prose*.[11] A few articles appeared in September, 1998 – in *The Guardian, The Independent* and *The Daily Telegraph* – discussing the merits of the Powys canon. Craig Brown, in a piece on obscure writers, said that Powys being neglected was part of his appeal, which he might lose if he became famous.[12] Tracy Carns, of the American Overlook Press (owned by Peter Mayer, ex-head of Penguin), whose *A Glastonbury Romance* was selling well in paperback (in import), said in *The Guardian* that the millenium period could be the moment when Powys's works moved into the mainstream.[13] The Overlook *A Glastonbury Romance*, apparently a 'best-seller' at Waterstone's book chain, was also cited in T*he Independent*'s article, with quotes from George Steiner and Henry Miller. *The Guardian* also quoted admirers such as Miller ('my first living idol'), Steiner (*A Glastonbury Romance* is 'the only novel produced by an English writer that can fairly be compared with the fictions of Tolstoy and Dostoievsky'), and Martin Amis ('a monument of neglect'), and a negative view, from Edith Sitwell ('I suppose that Messrs Powys were the first writers who experimented in deliberately boring their readers'). Powys was hailed as a 'New Age' writer fifty years before such ideas became fashionable. According to Waterstone's, Powys's books were chiming with those interested in the 'mind, body, spirit' section of the bookshop. 'It is no great surprise, perhaps, that thousands of baby-boomer readers who grew up with J.R.R. Tolkien should now want to spend their mature adulthood with the sprawling chronicles of Powys' wrote the correspondent. Stephen Moss noted that none of Powys's major works were currently in print in the UK; and none of his works were available from a major British publisher (op. cit.). *Weymouth Sands* was due to be published by the Overlook Press in 1999, with *Wolf Solent* also being re-issued in 1999. Vintage put out *Wolf Solent* in the US in November, 1998. On 13 September, 1998, Powys was, surprisingly, the subject of a short discussion on BBC Radio 4's flagship *Today* news programme, featuring Belinda Humfrey and Tracy Carns. Earlier in the year, BBC Radio 4 had broadcast an afternoon play based on the letters of Powys and Wilkinson, concerning the famous love triangle between Powys, Wilkinson and Frances Gregg. Commentators such as Wilkinson's son Oliver also appeared. Also in 1998, a short piece on *A Glastonbury Romance* by Herbert Williams was shown on HTV, concentrating on the spiritual, 'New Age' aspects of the novel.

Powys has often been published by individual admirers and smaller publishers, such as Jeffrey Kwinter and his Village Press in the 1970s, Malcolm Elwin and Macdonald, University of Wales Press, Enitharmon Press, Greymitre

Books, and more recently Cecil Woolf and Carcanet Press, and the Overlook Press and Colgate University Press in the US. The university presses and small presses are doing well in publishing Powys (often with subsidy, as with Carcanet's/ St Martin's Press's/ Alyscamps's Arts Council-funded *Petrushka and the Dancer*), but the audience for Powys via this route is limited. Ultimately, there is only one reason why publishers won't publish John Cowper Powys: they think he won't sell. Yet Powy's fiction delivers elements and pleasures that publishers and readers ask for, such as: strong narratives; extraordinary events (Porius's battle with the giant, for example); sex (Powys has lots of that, including, according to Wilson Knight, one of the best descriptions of sexual rapture in literature in *A Glastonbury Romance*); gossip (Powys's fiction has hundreds of social observations and dialogues); humour; intriguing characters.

Other authors of a similar generation or type as John Cowper Powys (such as Thomas Hardy and D.H. Lawrence) have their works made into films, television adaptions, theatre and radio plays; are set books in schools; are published expertly and in large amounts; and have special numbers of learned journals devoted to them. Why not Powys also? Perhaps one doesn't wish Powys to be turned into a 'heritage' author, like Thomas Hardy or Emily Brontë, who have tours, holidays, hotels and merchandizing based on them. There is one thing that could work wonders for John Cowper Powys's sales: a television adaption. Even if the Powys adaption were made by the BBC, with their customary attention to detail, it would probably have little to do with the original novels (the recent Jane Austen craze was sparked off by shoddy, sensationalized TV adaptions; ditto with Dickens, Trollope, Hardy and Eliot). But it might raise Powys's profile enormously, and encourage a few more people to seek out his books. (Imagine, though, a really good film version of Powys – *Wolf Solent* or *Owen Glendower* made by Ingmar Bergman or Werner Herzog, say: what a treat that might be).

And so to these essays: H.W. Fawkner's essay "Venus" explores issues of reading, movement, love and sex, the 'amorous self', and one of the main themes in Fawkner's recent Powys criticism, affectivity. Fawkner explores the beginning of *A Glastonbury Romance*, from its (in)famous opening paragraphs invoking solar and cosmic consciousness and the First Cause, to the East

Anglian sequence and first chapters. Fawkner's recent complex, idiosyncratic work on Powys has proved among the most challenging and insightful.

Ian Hughes looks at the genre of Powys's novels, and how the philosophical romances were influenced by Walter Pater's *Marius the Epicurean*. Janina Nordius discusses the crucial Powys theme of (transcendental) solitude in the key novel of the Powys-self alone, *Wolf Solent* (Wolf calls his 'under-life' his 'mythology' or 'life-illusion', his 'sinking into his soul'). Nordius brings in ideas (such as the 'philosophy of solitude' and the 'ichthyosaurian ego') from one of Powys's most accessible philosophical books, *In Defence of Sensuality*, written around the same time as *Wolf Solent* (1929-1930). Nordius also draws on Powys's philosophical works *A Philosophy of Solitude* and *The Complex Vision*. In Nordius's interpretation, the crucial struggle of Wolf to maintain his 'mythology' is related to issues such as sainthood, suffering and escape. Joe Boulter's essay concentrates on the affinities between modernism and post-modernism, pragmatism and deconstruction, in one of Powys's late novels, *The Inmates* (1952), via thinkers such as William James, Michel Foucault, Gilles Deleuze and Félix Guattari. Boulter also analyzes the theme of insanity and its relation to subjectivity.

This book is the first in a new series of collections of essays on John Cowper Powys.[14]

NOTES

1. However, in 1999, Penguin announced plans to publish *A Glastonbury Romance* in July, 1999, *Weymouth Sands* in March, 2000, and *Wolf Solent* in May, 2000. Also, a BBC documentary was apparently in progress (The Powys Society Newsletter, 37, July, 1999).

2. G. Wilson Knight: *Neglected Powers*, Routledge & Kegan Paul, 1972, 191.

3. H.W. Fawkner: *The Ecstatic World of John Cowper Powys*, Associated University Press, 1986, 220.

4. Penelope Shuttle: "John Cowper Powys", *The Powys Society Newsletter*, 31, July, 1997.

5. John Bayley: "A Polyindividuated Privacy", *The Powys Journal*, 1, 1991, 133.

6. See Gayatri Chakravorty Spivak: "French feminism in an international frame", *Yale French Studies*, 62, 1981.

7. John Hodgson: "Chance Groupings: An Anatomy of Ecstasy", *The Powys Journal*, 7, 1997, 14.

8. H.W. Fawkner: "The Manifestation of Affectivity: John Cowper Powys and Pure Romance", *The Powys Journal*, 7, 1997, 27.

9. J. Bayley, 1991, op.cit., 128.

10. W. Allen: *Tradition and Dream*, Phoenix, 1964, 71.

11. C. Woodhead: *The Sunday Telegraph*, 11 Sept, 1998.

12. C. Brown. "Private passions of obscure authors", *The Daily Telegraph*, 23 Sept, 1998

13. 7. S. Moss: "US revives 'forgotten' novelist's reputation", *The Guardian*, 16 Sept, 1998

14. People interested in contributing, please write to: Crescent Moon Publishing, P.O. Box 393, Maidstone, Kent, ME14 5XU, U.K.

JANINA NORDIUS
Wolf Solent: Towards a Discourse of Solitude[1]

All of John Cowper Powys's major novels are informed by an urge to explore the notion of solitude and its manifestations in human life – an inquiry which eventually led him to develop and articulate what he was to call his "philosophy of solitude." Yet although Powys was to make this construct the title of one of his essays – *A Philosophy of Solitude* (1933), together with the earlier *In Defence of Sensuality* (1930) his main platform for setting down his new philosophy in explicit terms[2] – the process of developing a discourse of solitude is, as intimated, something we can see taking place in all his texts of this period, fiction and "non-fiction" alike. The novels, in this process, become important sites for testing the new discourse of solitude against other, competing ones. As is my aim to show here, we can see this negotiation between discourses going on as early as in *Wolf Solent* (1929),[3] despite the fact that this novel was published a year before the first of the two essays mentioned above.

The personal philosophy that Powys articulated in *In Defence of Sensuality* and *A Philosophy of Solitude* can be summed up like this: rather than trying to escape our "inherent loneliness" by indulging in what Powys calls "drifting, brainless gregariousness" (PS, 45), we ought instead to accept it – "and not only accept it, but find our unique and singular happiness in it" (PS, 43). To Powys, such "singular happiness" is to be found not only in physical seclusion but, above all, in the experience of solitude as "a spiritual state" (DS, 124), a state which may be attained if we let ourselves sink down into the contemplation of our sensual impressions, or, as he writes, into "the contemplation of what we choose to select out of what surrounds us" (DS, 227-28). This state of contemplation he describes as "an erotic embrace of the not-self by the self" (PS, 88), a state of "solitary reciprocity" with the surrounding universe (DS, 32; PS, 90-91) – obviously, then, what we might call a *transcendental* state of solitude, although free from the theocentric connotations that often go with the word.

An important aim of Powys's philosophy is to develop a strategy for producing such moments of transcendental solitude by an act of will – a strategy he sums up in the "magic formula" which he coins in *In Defence of Sensuality*: "Enjoy – defy – forget" (277). The first step in such a process, Powys says, is one of forgetting "*what [we] decide to forget*" (DS, 29) – "our domestic worries, our money worries, our emotional worries, together with all those unbearable horrors that no effort of ours can affect" (PS, 115). Instead of letting itself be swamped by such worries, the solitary self should "deliberately concentrate" its energies on "the simplest of its causes for contentment" (DS, 37), by "giv[ing] itself up to a deep physical-psychic enjoyment of the thought of air, sun, earth, water, sky, warmth, food, amorous pleasure" – that is, the enjoyment of simply being alive (DS, 37). Importantly though, Powys stresses, this mental embrace is not just an act of self-abandonment but, at the same time, an act of defiance:

> It is in my power to gather up my forces and embrace this universe, represented by these material elements about me. It is in my power to assert my nature, my inmost being, against these things, upon these things. It is my power... to feel, as I stretch out my spirit towards them, that I am embracing, and yet defying, the whole material world! (PS, 92)

As hinted, then, the beginnings of this philosophy of solitude can be traced back to *Wolf Solent*, a novel which in this respect constitutes a radical re-examination of the attitude to solitude found in Powys's previous work. In his first book of popular philosophy, *The Complex Vision* (1920),[4] "the isolated loneliness of our deepest self" (CV, 92) is seen as an obstacle rather than a passport to blissful fulfilment; and in the four novels that preceded *Wolf Solent*,[5] the condition of being alone is represented as mainly involving problems – as a social handicap or as the lonely individual's striving for mastery over others or for power in the world, conditions equally detrimental in their respective ways to human happiness. However, although instances of similarly problematic solitude continue to haunt Powys's fictional worlds, we can nevertheless sense, from *Wolf Solent* on, a new acceptance and a new affirmation of solitude; and as a result, his fictional representation of such states acquires a new complexity and dynamics. Conceived, then, at a period of intellectual reorientation,[6] *Wolf Solent* may well be seen, in John Hodgson's words, as "a guide for Powys himself... bringing to disordered and semi-conscious mental states the clarity which comes with articulation; it is the resulting 'map' brought home after a period of self-exploration."[7] What is articulated is, as I have suggested, a provisional version of Powys's philosophy of solitude; and it is this process of articulation – which at times follows a rather meandering path – that is the main theme of *Wolf Solent*.

My concern in this essay is thus to situate *Wolf Solent* on the scale of development of Powys's personal philosophy. By pointing to a central division in Wolf's "mythology" (his personal life-illusion), I shall argue that in the struggle for hegemony between its two constituents, discussed here as the "philosophy of the saint" and the "philosophy of the ichthyosaurus," lies the seed not only of a new beginning for the protagonist but also of Powys's gradual articulation of his philosophy of solitude. When the "philosophy of the saint" proves untenable as an approach to life, Wolf's mythology dies; but the "new birth" (625) that results from his subsequent wholehearted acceptance of the "philosophy of the ichthyosaurus" means, in practice, his adopting of a philosophy very close to what was later to emerge as Powys's philosophy of solitude.

From the very first sentence of the novel, Wolf's eagerness for solitude is emphasised. We meet him praising his "good luck" at having "found a compartment to himself" in the train for Dorset, because being thus alone will enable him to "indulge in... an orgy of concentrated thought" (13). Indeed, it is both his fondness for actual, physical solitude and his inclination to mental withdrawals that make this character such a "lone wolf." His most guarded treasure is an aspect of his inner life which he thinks of as his "mythology" (19-20) – a secret space of solitude which provides the scene for his most exalted moments. How to preserve this space intact from the onslaughts of external reality is his greatest concern when he plunges into Dorset life, and it is, indeed, around this dilemma that most of the drama in the novel centres.

What is ultimately the subject of the novel's inquiry into Wolf's mythology is a felt conflict that haunts all Powys's writings about solitude during the late 20s and early 30s. This is the conflict between, on the one hand, the individual's need for solitary withdrawal – for the consolidation and a possible transcendence of self – and, on the other, the ineluctable and factual presence of suffering in the world around him. To Powys, the question how far we ought to sympathise with suffering becomes an acute ethical problem: a conflict, on the individual level, between solitude and commitment. It is this problem that Powys formulates in the question prefacing *In Defence of Sensuality*: "How far has the individual the right to be what is called 'selfish'? How far has he the right to concentrate on his own solitary awareness of existence and make this alone his life-purpose?" In the novels, manifestations of "suffering" occur on two levels: a general, universal – and rather abstract – one, and a personal level, often represented by the Powys-hero's closest relations – lovers, family, friends. In *Wolf Solent*, the former level is represented by a face Wolf glimpses on the Waterloo steps on leaving London, a face which to him comes to represent universal suffering, and which he on a later occasion associates with Christ (617), the archetypal "symbol of vicarious suffering."[8] Yet, as it turns out, it is the personal level which will present the most serious threats to his mythology.

This "mythology," cherished by Wolf as the most precious thing in his life, is a sensation of inner solitude, a mental withdrawal from the external world, which Wolf thinks of as "a certain trick he had of doing what he called 'sinking into his soul.'" This "mental device... supplied him with the secret substratum of his whole life" (19), and is linked to a sense of power. His mythology "consisted of a certain summoning-up, to the surface of his mind, of a subconscious magnetic power which... seemed prepared to answer such a summons" (20). Wolf visualises these magnetic impulses as "the expanding of great vegetable leaves over a still pool – leaves nourished by hushed noons, by liquid, transparent nights, by all the movements of the elements" (20).

However, Wolf's mythology is duplicitous. Although Wolf refers to it as one, and for all practical purposes treats it as such, the text of the novel shows us quite clearly that his mythology is really a blend of two disparate – and, in fact, incompatible – components. The narratorial remark that Wolf "was not rigid in his definitions" is clearly very much to the point (299). Thus, on the one hand the "mythology" is an ecstatic sensation, a state of transcendental solitude, far removed from rational thinking: "to abandon himself to the ecstasy of his 'mythology'" (414) is, to Wolf, the epitome of happiness (416); and ecstasy is, as H. W. Fawkner has discussed, non-dualistic and non-dialectical.[9] But, on the other hand, Wolf's mythology also contains a very conspicuous element of moral dualism, a dialectical struggle between Good and Evil:

> This secret practice [of sinking into his soul] was always accompanied by an arrogant mental idea – the idea, namely, that he was taking part in some occult cosmic struggle – some struggle between what he liked to think of as "good" and what he liked to think of as "evil" in those remote depths. (20)

The duplicity in Wolf's mythology seems to reflect, although in a somewhat perverted form, a tension between two different ideologies (or, to focus on the linguistic representation of these ideologies, two contending discourses) that we can detect in Powys's writing at the time of *Wolf Solent* and the following years (it is especially noticeable in *In Defence of Sensuality* and *A Glastonbury Romance*).[10] This is the tension between on the one hand the essentially non-moral (or beyond-moral) message of the philosophy of solitude that Powys was to develop in explicit terms in *In Defence of Sensuality*, and, on the other hand, an inability – or unwillingness – to rid himself of the moral imperative always to be good which is such an integral part of our Christian cultural heritage. The transcendental states of solitude that Powys's philosophy aims at are beyond-moral because in such ecstatic or near-mystical states duality is momentarily suspended (and any kind of moral awareness necessarily involves dualism). But we can also trace a clear debt to Nietzsche in the philosophy's rejection of the all-too-human which is "slowly assassinating all calm ecstatic happiness" (DS, 9). In *In Defence of Sensuality* the tension between, in very rough terms, the "Christian" and the "Nietzscheinspired" ideologies can be observed in the distinction which Powys makes between the "saint" and the "ichthyosaurus-ego."[11]

The notions of the ichthyosaurus-ego and the saint are, basically, two different ways of responding to the overriding existential dualism between happiness and suffering touched upon above, which is so foregrounded in Powys's writing of this period. In *In Defence of Sensuality*, Powys translates this existential dualism into a moral dualism – into the opposition between the cosmic forces of Good and Evil, the two faces of the double-natured First Cause: "This dualism sinks down to the very bottom of the cosmic pond, and doubtless extends... not merely to the fish down there, but to the subaqueous vegetation as well!" (DS, 127). It is the same idea of "an extreme dualism... descending to the profoundest gulfs of being, a dualism in which every living thing was compelled to take part" (WoS, 299) that Wolf gives expression to in the lines quoted above. For the solitary self, seeking to adjust itself to this dualistic world, there are only two alternatives, writes Powys in *In Defence of Sensuality*. "One is the philosophy of the ichthyosaurus, and the other is the philosophy of the saint" (DS, 253).

The "ichthyosaurus-ego" is the term Powys uses in *In Defence of Sensuality* for the "mingling in our 'I am I' of... [the] sub-human and super-human elements" he claims can be found in every human being (DS, 9). Whereas the ichthyosaurus-ego thus "exists in every man, woman, and child" (DS, 127), to be a "saint" is a highly unusual condition (DS, 62). The saint "has never hardened his heart" (DS, 63) to the appeals of other beings, and therefore he is able to enjoy the feeling "*of being free from remorse*" (DS, 62), that is, he is free from the "sense of being responsible for the cruelty in the system of things" (DS, 63). To be a "saint," then, means "to devote your life, by giving up the satisfaction of personal desires, to the alleviation of all sentient suffering" (DS, 251; see also 253). Although Powys stresses that being a saint in this sense does not depend "on any definite religious belief," not even "on believing in God" (DS, 63),[12] the Christian charity message is nevertheless unmistakable. The rest of us, he writes – those of us who do not live up to the infinite goodness of the saint – cannot but recognise that we must be implicated in "the cruelty in the system of things" and thus accept our share of remorse: "below our excitements and distractions, [we] carry a deep wedge of rankling shame, a queer dark wedge... in the very midriff of our being" (DS, 62-63). For us to cope with life, Powys argues, there remains only the other alternative, that is, the philosophy of the ichthyosaurus. This philosophy means "to try to *forget* the suffering as completely as you can, and devote your life to a defiant enjoyment of as much happiness, *of a certain very especial and particular kind,* as you can snatch or can create" (DS, 251-52; emphasis on "forget" mine). It is this ichthyosaurian philosophy with its motto "Enjoy – defy – forget" (DS, 277) that constitutes the core of what was later to become Powys's philosophy of solitude.

The key word here is "forget." This is Powys's way of resolving or, rather, bypassing the conflict between a "moral conscience"[13] and the beyond-moral mystic-sensuous enjoyment that can be found in the transcendental solitude that his philosophy sets out to aim at. To "forget" is an excellent way of "having it both ways" (WoS, 466). The gist of the distinction between the ichthyosaurian and the saintly attitude to life seems to be, then, that while the ichthyosaurus may forget both the sufferings of others and his own remorse, the saint (in no need to forget a remorse he does not feel) *does not allow* himself to forget the sufferings of others, always trying to do good by relieving the causes of their distress before he thinks of himself (DS, 64). In other words, while the ichthyosaurus allows himself to forget about the dualisms of life – at least now and again – the saint is always alert to them.

These are, then, the two "ideal" positions that can be extracted from Powys's discussion of the saint and the ichthyosaurus in *In Defence of Sensuality*, and it is these two attitudes to life, thus defined, that I will draw on in my discussion of *Wolf Solent*'s mythology. Let me point out at once, however, that Powys's use of these two concepts in his writings of the period is far from consistent. He is no more rigid in his definitions than is Wolf, and the distinction between the saint and the ichthyosaurus becomes at times so blurred as to almost collapse. That the ichthyosaurus is encouraged to be good to the best of his abilities (DS, 127), and even to debouch "now and again into the 'rarefied air' of that noble life of the Saint which... it presumes to admire" (DS, 252), may be permissible; as has just been mentioned, the hallmark of the ichthyosaurus is to have it both ways. Likewise we may accept that the saint, too, regards the enjoyment of transcendental solitude as a most "thrilling happiness" which he does everything to evoke – but, importantly, "first for others," and only "then for himself" (DS, 63-64). But when we are told, elsewhere, that even a "saint" must sometimes forget his "acts of social kindness" in order to have "some moments of... [his] own",[14] we may well ask ourselves what difference there remains. The way I read Powys's wavering on this point is simply as an indication of the impracticability of sainthood as soon as we try to envisage it in some detail – implying, perhaps that "sainthood" may be best thought of as an idea – or an "ideal." Clearly, however, Powys's ambivalence here also points to the fact that the relation of solitude to ethics was a problem with which he was in the process of grappling, and in regard to which he had not yet found or articulated his "final" standpoint.

The reason why I nevertheless choose to work with this distinction, in spite of its obvious instability, is that it seems to me the most genuine expression of the ideological shift that is on its way in Powys's writing during this period. While the ichthyosaurus, as we have seen, represents Powys's new philosophy of solitude, the saint is a figure of long standing in his work. As early as 1916 he published a poem called 'The Last Saint', whose motto was given as "Until ye die hold charity / More potent than the sword."[15] And although the term is not explicitly used in *Wolf Solent*, it does indeed occur in Powys's next novel, *A Glastonbury Romance*, where the philosophy of the saint is explicitly contrasted to that of the ichthyosaurus.

I shall argue, then, that the duplicity in Wolf's mythology can be discussed in terms of a clash between these two "philosophies." Put simply, while Wolf is shown to be a practising "ichthyosaurus," his idea of himself as a staunch and unfailing champion of good against evil seems to reveal an ambition similar to that which Powys ascribes to the saint in *In Defence of Sensuality*.[16] I say 'seems to', because obviously this "sainthood" that I assign to Wolf is only a mock sainthood; his championship of the good is a perversion of the saintly ideals of *In Defence of Sensuality*, since it remains a mere idea without empirical foundation. There is never a question of his "giving up the satisfaction of personal desires" (DS, 251) in order to alleviate the sufferings of others; on the contrary, it is stated quite clearly that "his 'mythology'... had no outlet in any sort of action. It was limited entirely to a secret sensation in his own mind" (20). (That this may involve a problem does not bother Wolf, since he does not articulate the details of his mythology; he is perfectly content to leave the "essence" of his struggle against evil "vague and obscure", 299). Nor,

I would like to emphasise again, is the term "saint" ever used in the novel to describe this moral element in Wolf's mythology. Bearing these reservations in mind, I shall nevertheless contend that through his claim to absolute goodness Wolf puts himself in the same precarious situation as the saint of *In Defence of Sensuality*, and that, therefore, an analysis of his situation in terms of the clashing philosophies of the saint and the ichthyosaurus will be profitable.

Ultimately, both sides of Wolf's mythology – his mock "sainthood" and his "ichthyosaurian" life alike – depend on his relation to the external world, although as we shall see they do so in different ways. Wolf's mythology is an escape from the reality of other people into his own private world. The "mythology" is "his *escape from life*, his *escape* into a world where machinery could not reach him, his *escape* into a deep, green, lovely world where thoughts unfolded themselves like large, beautiful leaves growing out of fathoms of blue-green water" (544; emphasis mine). Having thus escaped, his mythology becomes his "true reality":

> Outward things... were to him like faintly-limned images in a mirror, the *true reality* of which lay all the while in his mind – in these hushed, expanding leaves – in this secret vegetation – the roots of whose being hid themselves beneath the dark waters of his consciousness. (20-21; emphasis mine)

However, although no such thing is ever articulated, we can see that Wolf's escapes into the solitude of his mythology are really of two different kinds – the defensive and protective escapes of the mock saint, and the escapes of the ichthyosaurus which are motored by "forgetting" and "enjoying" (that is, escapes into transcendental solitude). The escapes of the mock saint are marked by an awareness of antagonistic dualism – the antagonism between the "true reality" of his mythology and the "*real reality*" of other people, "the reality his mother lived in" (546) – but also, as we have seen, the antagonism inherent in his idea of a dualistic struggle between good and evil. "Real reality" is where "evil" resides: most conspicuously exemplified by the lechery of his employer and the bookseller Mr Malakite, and the necrophilia Wolf suspects his employer Urquhart of. But while his mythology protects him from external "real reality," it is also threatened by it. As Wolf approaches Dorset on the train, he fears for the integrity of his mythology. He fears that "his furtive, private, hidden existence" (32) will be invaded by people belonging to "real reality." He fears that "these unknown people... would be able to do what no outward events had yet done – break up this mirror of half-reality and drop great stones of real reality... among those dark waters and that mental foliage" (21). What is most obviously at risk of being broken up here is of course Wolf's illusion of himself as permanently siding with the good. *Any* encounter with outside social or interpersonal reality is liable to put such an absolutist claim to shame and thus undermine the foundations of his mythology (and this, as we shall see, is exactly what happens in the novel). As a rather desperate measure against this fear of outside reality, Wolf occasionally chooses to deny that it is there at all, by lapsing into sheer solipsism: "I don't believe in any reality.... Everything *is* as I myself create it. I am the wretched demiurge of the whole spectacle.... Alone... alone... alone!" (489; first ellipsis mine, other punctuation Powys's).

As has already been intimated, however, the escapes from life that Wolf associates with his mythology are not limited to these defensive retreats into the "charmed circle" of his own "private consciousness" (20) where he can cultivate duality at leisure. Sometimes his escapes are explicitly represented as taking him a step further, transporting him to an ecstatic state of transcendental solitude, which in its most elated forms is represented as being like the "entrance into an unknown dimension" (151). In such states, dualistic thinking is momentarily forgotten. These are the kind of escapes that Powys's philosophy of solitude urges the ichthyosaurus-ego to strive for, and when Wolf reaches this state he stops thinking in words – the leaves and blue-green water of his mythology becoming a wordless representation of his non-dimensional space of transcendental solitude. Thus, while the "saintly" Wolf is anxious to stay away from the reality of other people in order to protect his moral dualism, the ichthyosaurian Wolf is able to escape also from his ordinary defensive self, private though it may be, and *forget* about dualism.

Wolf is not aware, however, of the twofold nature of his mythology. Since he does not articulate it in rational terms, he does not realise what "a jumbled parcel of odd and often self-contradictory notions" his inner life is.[17] It is perhaps not surprising, therefore, that in spite of his notion of himself as a full-time champion of the good, he is not only "forgetful" as an ichthyosaurus, but also, sometimes, explicitly thinks of himself and his mythology in ichthyosaurian terms. On one occasion, he literally thinks of himself as having "the sensations of an ichthyosaurus" (291); furthermore, reptilian images are legion in descriptions of "mythological" states (e.g. 16, 17) (the term "ichthyosaurus-ego" being chosen, as Powys stresses in *In Defence of Sensuality*, "to emphasize the remote vegetable-reptile-saurian background of the human soul," DS 9). Watching "a great alder-root that curved snake-like" over a river-bank, Wolf seems to detect in this "serpent of vegetation" an "image of his own secretive life, craftily forcing its way forward" towards the "ecstasy he aimed at" (152-53). Significantly, the "intoxicating enlargement of personality that used to come to him from imagining himself a sort of demiurgic force" (16) is thought, by Wolf, to be "just that sort of enlargement he experienced" when he falls back upon "a crafty, elusive cunning of his own, a cunning both slippery and serpentine" (16).

As C. A. Coates has pointed out, the "ichthyosaurus ego" has associations with fish as well, and Wolf's mythology is from early on also expressed in fish imagery: "Wolf felt the familiar mystic sensation surging up even now from its hidden retreat. Up, up it rose, like some great moonlight-coloured fish from fathomless watery depths" (39; see also 502-3).[18] Fish is, of course, another figure of the "sub-human' and it is mainly as such, I would argue, that it should be seen here. Still, since the fish is also a traditional symbol of Christ, we may, if so inclined, see this juxtaposition of fish and snake in the figure of the ichthyosaurus as yet another expression of its inclination to have it both ways – bypassing either-or dualism by going beyond both good and evil.[19]

The "ichthyosaurian" side of Wolf's mythology is also apparent when we consider the specific nature of his escapes into transcendental solitude. They are expressly represented as *selective* in relation to the external world (just as are the escapes of the ichthyosaurus in *In Defence of Sensuality*). That is to say, Wolf does not only escape away from the dialectics and dualisms of ordinary social reality, but in doing so he turns instead to a mental embrace of material reality. His ecstasies are explicitly said to be achieved through solitary reciprocity with the inanimate. Clearly, such reciprocity is a far cry from the solipsism which, as we saw, his mock-saintly aspect would sometimes land him in. It is when, for instance, Wolf "follow[s] the wraith-like vapours of autumn as they drifted over the lanes and hills, and give[s] himself up with a large forgetfulness of everything else, to his sensuous-mystical mythology" that he experiences the "moments of ecstasy" (406-7) which give spiritual nourishment to his daily life. Or, when watching a patch of blue sky glimpsed through filmy clouds (151), Wolf experiences a "moment of ecstasy" (152) as "ever more nearly and more nearly what he saw became what he imagined" (152). The "embrace" of matter becomes almost palpable here: that "incredible patch of blue" seems to Wolf like "something into which he could plunge his hands and draw them forth again, filled like overflowing cups with the very ichor of happiness" (151). Again, it is this elated feeling of "*pure happiness*" that makes his mythology so precious to him: "this was the thing, he thought... after which his whole life was one obstinate quest" (151).

In the light of Wolf's explicit connecting of such experiences with his mythology, his claim, on another occasion, that the mental embrace of the inanimate which he thinks of as "*fetish-worship*" is something different from his mythology, may perhaps be ascribed to his general lack of articulate and "rigid" thinking. Fetish-worship is said to be his "normal attitude to life" (54), the philosophy "that remained with him during all the normal hours when his 'mythology' – his secret spiritual vice – lay quiescent" (54). Despite this declaration, however, the text inscribes Wolf's fetish-worship as a state not at all "normal', but as an ecstatic state, a state of solitary reciprocity, of exactly the same kind as those other instances of transcendental solitude we have just encountered. It "was a worship of all the separate, mysterious, living souls he approached: 'souls' of grass, trees, stones, animals, birds, fish; 'souls' of planetary bodies and of the bodies of men and women; the 'souls' even, of all manner of inanimate little things... ", and in watching these things, "he lost all thought of himself... Their beauty held him in a magical enchantment; and between his soul and the 'soul,' as it were, of whatever it was he happened to be regarding, there seemed to be established a tremulous and subtle reciprocity" (54-55).

Wolf's mental fusion of two visions as incompatible as those of the ichthyosaurus and the mock-saint makes the result of this fusion – his "mythology" – a rather fragile construct. As has already been pointed out, it can survive only because it is neither articulated nor tested against external "real reality" (546)

– its vulnerable part being, of course, Wolf's illusion of himself as an infallible champion of the good. When eventually this part of his life-illusion collapses, he thinks of his whole "mythology" as dead, and from this point onward, it is his gradual awakening to the duplicity of his former mythology and his articulation of a new attitude to life that is the focus of the novel. In this process of self-discovery it is significant – and ironic – that what grieves Wolf most in thinking of his lost mythology is the loss of its ecstatic potential. "His 'mythology' would never help him again. That ecstasy, that escape from reality, was gone" (534). Yet, his realisation, after a brief period of crisis, that this potential is, after all, not *gone* – that it resides in his capacity to enjoy his sensations rather than in his moral dualism – clears the way for an unblurred acceptance of the philosophy of the ichthyosaurus, uncontaminated now by any aspirations to the absolute goodness of the saint.

Seen in a larger perspective, this acceptance by Wolf of the philosophy of the ichthyosaurus marks a similar turning-point in Powys's literary and philosophical production as a whole. Although I have employed here the notions of the saint and the ichthyosaurus, it is, as we remember, only after writing *Wolf Solent* that Powys articulates this distinction in explicit terms in *In Defence of Sensuality,* and is able to formulate the "ichthyosaurian" philosophy of solitude that would become so influential in his later writings. Yet without trying out his new discourse of solitude in *Wolf Solent,* such articulation might not have been possible.

What happens to promote Wolf's passage from mythology to philosophy of solitude, then, is this. Once arrived in Dorset, Wolf is no longer able to keep external "real reality" (546) at bay as he had evidently been able to do before. A major reason for this is his falling in love – first with the physically attractive Gerda, whom he marries, and then with the intellectual and "androgynous"-looking Christie Malakite (83), to whom Wolf seems even more attracted. "Love was a possessive, feverish, exacting emotion. It demanded a response. It called for mutual activity. It entailed responsibility" (55). Through love, Wolf becomes involved in "real reality", and this reality makes a twofold attack upon his mythology. It provides an occasion for him to spend the night with Christie Malakite, and it offers him a cheque for £200 for finishing a pornographic book for his employer, a project which he had already decided to give up (406). Accepting either of these "offers" would mean sacrificing his moral conscience and entail the killing of his mythology (426). Wolf would have "to outrage... the very core of his nature! That hidden struggle between some mysterious Good and some mysterious Evil, into which all his ecstasies had merged, how could it go on after this?" (421).

It is when Wolf is faced with the need to make decisions – "real" dualistic choices between either accepting what he is offered or not – that his wholesale championship of the good reveals its untenability. Being forced to define which option is the "good" one and which is the "evil", he realises that in real life, things are not that simple and clear-cut. Decisions are not always ideally between good and evil, but more often between just bad and bad. Rejecting the offers he has been given seems as bad as accepting them. Sacrificing Christie would mean seriously hurting her feelings and also giving up his "only one single, simple, and world-deep craving – the craving to spend his days and his nights with that other mysterious and mortal consciousness, entitled Christie Malakite" (288). Giving up the cheque for £200 would leave Gerda sorely disappointed and most likely entail a break with her. Thus, whichever way he turns, he is implicated in "evil", and when Wolf realises this, his whole mythology collapses (534, 544). "'Reality has beaten me,' he said to himself" (572). "His 'mythology,' whatever it had been, *was dead*" (631).

The insight that he cannot avoid being implicated in "evil" plunges Wolf into a temporary depressive crisis. In the terminology of *In Defence of Sensuality*, we might say that he is struck with *remorse*, which he does not know how to handle, since he has been protected from this feeling by his conviction of his own "goodness." He emerges from his crisis, however, through a series of "insights" of different kinds, insights that are glimpsed and forgotten a number of times before they finally sink in, but which nonetheless can be roughly outlined as follows: after having first accepted intellectually that he is not a "saint" who can live free from remorse, he learns to articulate, in explicit terms, the philosophy of the ichthyosaurus that we have seen him practising all along. Parallel to this intellectual achievement occurs a rebirth of Wolf's capacity to enjoy the ecstatic states of transcendental solitude which were what he treasured so highly in his mythology.

To accept his implication in *the whole* of life is something Wolf learns from his mother, whose attitude here seems to comprise both stoicism and Nietzschean life-affirmation. To her, being part of life is not a dualistic option of being *either* good *or* bad. Rather, it means "that we all *have to be bad* sometimes... just as we all *have to be good* sometimes" (476; punctuation Powys's). What Wolf learns here is a Nietzschean "Yes to life", an "affirmation without reservation even of suffering, even of guilt, even of all that is strange and questionable in existence."[20]

But, importantly, mere acceptance is not enough. It is followed by yet another step, and it is in this step that Powys deliberately departs from Nietzsche.[21] This is the explicit articulation of the philosophy of the ichthyosaurus, and here too Wolf gets help from outside – from a person belonging to that "real reality" his mother lived in (546). Although Wolf, as we have seen, has been practising the art of forgetting this reality from the outset (in his escapes into transcendental solitude),[22] it is nevertheless as if the full significance of the word "forget" does not become a conscious awareness in him until at the end, after the death of his mythology, when he is faced with the problem of how to handle his remorse. It is Mr Malakite who teaches him that it is necessary sometimes to forget not only the horrors of life as such but also one's own part and the part of one's loved ones in them. The old man is dying from a fall down the stairs, which he blames on Christie, his daughter: "She pushed me down" (595). As the dying man falters, "for – ", "for – ", Wolf expects his last word to be "forgive!" (595). If it had, Malakite would indeed have behaved as would one of the saints of *In Defence of Sensuality*, because to forgive seems to be the privilege of those free from remorse.

Wolf's idea of forgiving as the privilege of the innocent is a result of his meeting with the only person in the novel who comes anywhere near the ideal of the saint, the very minor character Gaffer Barge. Barge's only characteristic is his "inborn", "heathen goodness" (625, 622), and his sheer minority prevents him from being implicated in any real life situations that might contaminate his goodness.[23] Barge is "an innocent", reflects Wolf, "so it may be permitted to *him* to forgive" (617).

However, Mr Malakite is no more a saint than is Wolf, and his last word is not "forgive" but "Forget!" (595). To Wolf, this explicit exhortation works as an eye-opener. To forget, he realises, is the only way to cope with remorse if we want to make life bearable. This (hitherto only instinctual) understanding now becomes an intellectually articulated insight, which Wolf makes into a conscious strategy, an instrument to be used at will. What Wolf formulates at the end of the novel is almost literally the "magic formula" of Powys's ichthyosaurian philosophy of solitude: "'There is no limit to the power of my will,' he thought, 'as long as I use it for two uses only... to forget and to enjoy!'" (631; punctuation Powys's).

Having thus intellectually both accepted and articulated this key notion of the philosophy of the ichthyosaurus, Wolf is anxious to pass it on to others. Most immediately this involves Christie (the alleged murderess),[24] because what he thinks is her suffering and remorse, Wolf makes his own. "There's only one thing for us to do if we're to endure life at all, Chris; and... and your father said the word himself before he died... He said 'forget,' Chris... From now on that is the word for us" (597; last two ellipses mine). On a less personal level, Wolf aims straight at the heart of sainthood by addressing its prime model, the archetype of vicarious suffering himself. In an imagined meeting with Christie's near-namesake, Christ (who merges here, in Wolf's imagination, with the man of the Waterloo steps), Wolf absolves him from the imperative to suffer with mankind: "You needn't suffer. I let you off. *You are allowed to forget*" (617).[25] And "once you've been told that you have the right to forget", Wolf tells Christ, "[a]ny secret life can be borne" (617).

It may be as an implicit result of this insight that Wolf is granted what he himself perceives of as a "blind new birth" (625); in the last pages of the novel, he is shown again to be able to enjoy the ecstasies of transcendental solitude which he thought lost with the death of his mythology. Yet this new birth is "blind", because although it may be linked, in the remote depths of his consciousness, to his rational understanding of the need to forget, there is, in its initial phase, nothing intellectual or rational *per se* about it. On the contrary, it is expressly represented as a non-intellectual, non-articulate experience that depends on his body rather than his mind – as something taking place virtually independently of the mental understanding we have just witnessed.

On the level of plot psychology, this split understanding of Wolf's can be put down to the nature of his depressive crisis, which is rendered as a felt separation of body and mind. For Wolf's mental understanding, the key notion was to "forget"; but "Chance" also causes "the earth to whisper some clue word into the ears of his flesh, a word that his *body* understood, though his mind was too humiliated to focus itself upon it" (619). This clue word is to be found in "his vegetable-animal identity, isolated, solitary" (593), in "his vegetable-animal integrity" (593) – that is to say, in the subhuman element within himself which is brought out in his mystic-sensuous communion with the material inanimate, rather than in the purely ideational sphere of his mind where his now lost "goodness" used to reside. It is when his body understands this clue word that he is again allowed to experience "a flowing reciprocity with that life that was far older than animal life" (625) – a sensation, then, which he experiences as "a kind of blind new birth" (625). But also here, when this new understanding is finally articulated, it is shown to be only a new discovery, and a new affirmation, of an old, never articulated intuition: "He recognized now that his secret motive of all these months... had been his faith in some vast earth-bound power within him that was stronger than the Christian miracle!" (625; cf. also e.g. 52).

Thus, both on a mental and a physical level, Wolf experiences how the philosophy of the ichthyosaurus outconquers that of the saint, and this twofold recognition makes him whole again: "Ah! His body and his soul were coming together again now!" (625). Recognising that what he is now able to acknowledge intellectually is only the implications of earlier experiences, he thinks of it as a change that "had taken place within him, a rearrangement, a readjustment of his ultimate vision, from which he could never again altogether recede" (630). This readjustment of vision involves also a new attitude to the super-human. The "supernatural" of his mythology – the antagonistic "either-or" dualism – with its debt to traditional Manichaean religion has ceased to appeal to him: "That sense of a supernatural struggle going on in the abysses, with the Good and the Evil so sharply opposed, had vanished from his mind. To the very core of life, things were more involved, more complicated than that!" (631). Instead, the divine is resituated in the "earthly solidity" of a glorious field of buttercups as Wolf, absorbed in the golden shades of the flowers, visualises the whole stretch of West country lying before him "as if it were itself one of the living personalities of his life" – as if it were, indeed, "a god!" (632).

On a broader scale, the "readjustment of vision" that Powys ascribes to his character here can also be seen to inform his own writing from this point on. It is in *Wolf Solent* that we can trace the first signs of the "philosophy of solitude" he was to articulate a few years later in *In Defence of Sensuality* and *A Philosophy of Solitude*, and it is in *Wolf Solent* that he first tries out the discourse of solitude that was to be so noticeable in all his great novels of the next two decades.

Part of this essay appeared in Janina Nordius's *"I Am Myself Alone": Solitude and Transcendence in John Cowper Powys*, Göteborg University Press, Sweden, 1997.

NOTES

1. The main part of this essay is based on an edited version of chapter two in my book *"I Am Myself Alone": Solitude and Transcendence in John Cowper Powys*, Gothenburg Studies in English 67 (Göteborg: Göteborg University, 1997).

2. *A Philosophy of Solitude* (1933; London: Village Press, 1974), when relevant abbreviated as PS in the following; *In Defence of Sensuality* (London: Gollancz, 1930), abbrevated as DS.

3. *Wolf Solent* (1929; Harmondsworth: Penguin, 1964); abbreviated as WoS when relevant.

4. *The Complex Vision* (1920; London: Village Press, 1975), abbreviated as CV when relevant.

5. *Wood and Stone* (1915); *Rodmoor* (1916); *After My Fashion* (written c. 1920; published posthumously in 1980); *Ducdame* (1925).

6. The novel was written during the years 1925-28; see Belinda Humfrey, "'Let Our Crooked Smokes Climb... From Our Bless'd Altars!': *Wolf Solent*: Designs, Writing, Achievement", *John Cowper Powys's Wolf Solent: Critical Studies*, ed. Belinda Humfrey (Cardiff: University of Wales Press, 1990), 2, 7, 11.

7. John Hodgson, "'A Victim of Self-Vivisection' – John Cowper Powys and *Wolf Solent*", Humfrey, JCP's *Wolf Solent* 33.

8. In his essay *The Art of Forgetting the Unpleasant* (1928; London: Village Press, 1974), Powys refers to "Jesus himself, who remains the supreme symbol of vicarious suffering carried to the limit" (9). (The distinction that Powys made elsewhere between the figure of "Jesus" and the figure of "Christ" – see, for instance, *The Complex Vision* 240 – may be of less relevance here).

9. H. W. Fawkner, "John Cowper Powys and Ontotheology", *Powys Review*, 23 [6.3] (1989), 39. See also Fawkner, *The Ecstatic World of John Cowper Powys* (Rutherford, NJ: Fairleigh Dickinson University Press, 1986), 29-39.

10. For a discussion of discourse and ideology, see e.g. Sara Mills, *Discourse, New Critical Idiom* (London: Routledge, 1997), 29-47.

11. The role of both Christ and Nietzsche in Powys's writings has been recognised by, for instance, G. Wilson Knight who devotes some space to Powys in his *Christ and Nietzsche: An Essay in Poetic Wisdom* (London: Staples, 1948). Powys himself has written on both: in *The Complex Vision* one chapter is called "The Figure of Christ", and he has essays on Nietzsche in *Visions and Revisions* (1915) and in *The Pleasures of Literature* (1938).

12. Nor does it imply "any rigid morality", whereby Powys is obviously referring to societal morality, stressing the saint's lenience "to every kind of sex-sensation" (DS, 63).

13. *The Art of Forgetting the Unpleasant*, 5.

14. *The Meaning of Culture* (1929; Westport, CT: Greenwood, 1979) 130-31.

15. 'The Last Saint' 11-12, *Wolf's Bane* (1916; London: Village Press, 1975), 40. In *Confessions of Two Brothers*, published the same year (1916; London: Browne, 1982), Powys writes: "I have a queer inexplicable penchant for a saint's life. How lovely to possess nothing, and to have no ties! How lovely to wander about from village to village, living on bread and milk, and working miracles!" (110). The idea of "saintliness" seems to have been "in the air" during these years; cf. William James's chapters on saintliness in *The Varieties*

of Religious Experience: A Study in Human Nature (London: Longmans, 1902; 1919). Referring, in his *Autobiography*, to William James as "a startling delight", Powys also relates an incident when he missed getting off the train because he was so absorbed in James's *Varieties of Religious Experience* (*Autobiography* [1934; London: Picador-Pan, 1982], 479).

16. Cf. Morine Krissdóttir who comments on this situation: "He has linked his soul... explicitly with the good and implicitly with Christianity" (*John Cowper Powys and the Magical Quest* [London: Macdonald, 1980] 68). Humfrey, in "'Let Our Crooked Smokes Climb", comments on "Wolf's alternative welcoming and shying away from Christian modes of life" (19).

17. Margaret Moran, "Creative Lies", Humfrey, *JCP's Wolf Solent*, 194.

18. C. A. Coates, *John Cowper Powys in Search of a Landscape* (London: Macmillan, 1982), 52-53.

19. Cf. G. Wilson Knight, *The Saturnian Quest: A Chart of the Prose Works of John Cowper Powys* (London: Methuen, 1964), 33.

20. Friedrich Nietzsche, *Ecco Homo: How One Becomes What One Is*, trans. by R. J. Hollingdale (Harmondsworth: Penguin, 1979), 80.

21. Powys was to comment on this departure from Nietzsche in *A Philosophy of Solitude* a few years later in his discussion on contemptus fati. Rather than accepting and loving the world in its totality, he argues, we should try to escape "with the calm, austere, exultant... expectancy of Matter itself" from what we cannot bear, that is, we should escape by acknowledging the sub-human (or material) element in ourselves (PS, 212).

22. Cf. his meditation, "The stream of life is made of little things... To forget the disgusting ones and fill yourself with the lovely ones... that's the secret" (WoS, 448; first ellipsis mine).

23. Barge is a "saint" only in the sense of *In Defence of Sensuality*, that is, quite irrespectively of any religious belief in God. This ought perhaps to be emphasised, in the light of Ben Jones's discussion of a perplexing misprint that appears in some of the later editions of *Wolf Solent*. Gaffer Barge's goodness, which in the Simon and Schuster and in the Cape editions is given as "heathenly" has been replaced by "heavenly" goodness (e.g. in the Penguin edition used in this study, see 631). Jones objects to this editorial piety and states: "The ending of *Wolf Solent* is heathen, and heathenly Barge helps to make it so"; see Ben Jones, "Who Converted Gaffer Barge?", *Powys Review*, 13 [4.1] (1983-84): 43. Certainly the ending of *Wolf Solent* is ichthyosaurianly heathen; the important point in my reading, however, is not whether Barge is heathenly or heavenly good, but just that he is good; and in this respect he cannot help appearing as a Powysian "saint."

24. For a discussion of this incident, see J. S. Rodman, "Plotting *Wolf Solent*", *Powys Review*, 26 [8.2] (1991): 14. Rodman argues the possibility "that Malakite was murdered by Christie and that the crime was premeditated and even skilfully planned" (16).

25. Again, this is only the conscious articulation of an old insight: the idea of vicarious suffering has already been dismissed as "wicked" by Wolf (WoS, 153).

H.W. FAWKNER
Venus: Phenomenology of the Beginning of Movement in *A Glastonbury Romance*

In *A Glastonbury Romance* movement is not a phenomenon among other phenomena. Movement is not situated in the work in the way that most of the work's units of reality are situated in it – for movement is not 'real' in the first place. There is a sense in which movement is real and a sense in which movement is more important than the real. The movement that is more important than 'real' movement may be referred to as *archi-movement*. In this essay, the word 'movement' will designate archi-movement and not simply movement in general as a simple mobility, displacement, or locomotion occurring in the world.

An innocent reader reading the first page of *A Glastonbury Romance* might get the superficial impression that the 'world' of this romance is planetary or astrological. The references to "the First Cause," to "the soul of the great blazing sun," and to "the uttermost stellar systems" seem to make romance galactic from the outset (21). This impression is misleading. One of the reasons for this is that a 'first' page of a literary work is not its beginning. Common sense believes that reading is a chronological experience, and that the novel is an art-form that unfolds in 'time.' Common sense views music, cinematography, and reading as lineal, and understands painting and sculpture as stationary, 'spatial.' If this were the case, a person picking up *A Glastonbury Romance*, holding it in both hands, would feel that the left hand holding the book was somehow closer than the right hand to 'the beginning' of the book. In point of fact, however, what I hold in my hand is *the book*. We read with our hands, never with our eyes. Even the act of reading novels on computer-screens is in essence manual rather than optical – for the novel carries within itself the sense of an originary manual presence, the sensation 'in it' that it belongs to the hands of a being who has decided to effectuate a reading. Since reading is manual-holistic rather than optical-intentional, since it is in an important sense blind, eyeless – the work's *true* 'first page' is not simply the one that is numerically anterior to all the rest. In beholding the manual comportment of a reader, we do not feel that the *life* of the reader's hands is expressed in the banal act of merely turning the page. The hands of the reader do not primarily turn pages. What I hold in my hands as I begin to read is not a series of pages, ordered numerically in a proper sequence. What I hold in my hands is a sense of things to come. That a sense of things to come could be held in my hands... this is the secret not only of the experience of reading but of the actual thrill of the novel as such. The 'first page' of *A Glastonbury Romance* is from this viewpoint not the first one that comes to view in the procession of ordered pagination. The 'first page' is instead that page which comes to hold a sway and pre-eminence over others. Anyone wishing to uncover the 'planetary' or 'astro-physical' build-up of *A Glastonbury Romance* will accordingly recognize that the 'first page' to offer a primary clue in this matter appears not at the beginning of chapter 1 but in the early parts of chapter 5, 'Whitelake Cottage.' This is the page which introduces the affectivity of "the great planet of the evening itself" – Venus (135).

The 'planetary' or 'astro-physical' in *A Glastonbury Romance* is the affective, and the planetary-affective *is movement*. *Movement* is a significant clue to the work's main point of sustained focus – the nature, origin, and godlikeness of love in a Christian civilization. The superficial reader might prematurely want to accept the childish and obvious reading which the opening page seems to prompt; a reading in which we understand various characters as coming under the 'influence' of various heavenly bodies at various times in their lives and at various moments during the day. However, *movement* as the astro-physical display of the 'planetary' motion of affects does not primarily point to planet-to-planet interactivity or to planet-to-person transaction. *Movement*, whether it be planetary, transplanetary, or subplanetary, points to itself. In *A Glastonbury Romance* this pointing-to-itself of movement is manifested *as* the inter-planetary, and *as* the interpersonal. So there are not first planets, individuals, and affects – and then only subsequently movement. On the contrary, there is first movement... and only in and as the diffusion of movement's peculiar auto-affectivty is there an 'outward' production of heavenly and earthly bodies, heavenly and earthly interactivity, heavenly and earthly drama, heavenly and earthly beings.

But what is movement? In order to answer this question, we first need to address the question of transfer. On many occasions in *A Glastonbury Romance*, we are informed that a power or affect is transferred from one point in the universe to another. Thus the planet Venus transfers love to Nell Zoyland. "Some mysterious vibration had passed between the girl and that white planet in the western sky" (138). "She permitted Aphrodite to be her guide" (139). The goddess Aphrodite/ Venus has "persuaded" Nell not to discontinue the erotic simultaneity in which she loves her husband, Will Zoyland, but also her lover, Sam Dekker. However, the site of the reception of the love-force transferred from Venus is not Nell herself, not even her heart, but "some *remote place* in her heart" (138; emphasis added). The planet Venus is remote, but so also is the "remote place" *on this side* of Nell Zoyland. Venus is far away. "Whiter than Whitelake stream, whiter even than the girl's face, this celestial luminary... emerged now from the cloudy western lake wherein the sun had vanished" (135). But Nell Zoyland too is far away. This other farawayness is not exterior; nor is it interior. The other farawayness is *on this side* of interiority. If the planet Venus is remote and "celestial," so also is its point of impact, so also is the affect Venus (love as such), so also is the "place in her heart" which is not her heart but the heart-felt "place" in the heart which is "remote," which is a "hidden chamber there" (138). Nell Zoyland has a heart, a sensitivity, a capacity for loving; but she also has a heart *on this side* of her heart, a love *on this side* of her capacity to love. This other remoteness has nothing whatsoever to do with transcendency. It is the immanent remoteness which permits the 'planetary' (in this case Venus, love) to be something other than galactic, astro-physical, horizontal, cosmic.

In *A Glastonbury Romance* there is a perpetual showing of a planetary immanency. This planetary immanency is always movement – and always movement as the arising without transfer of the planetary immanency in itself. What is 'transferred' to Nell Zoyland 'from' Venus (from the possibility of love in general and as such) is paradoxically that which obviates transfer in the first place. To be 'influenced' by the goddess of love is to come under the spell of that which effortlessly passes through itself. "A long relaxed shiver of nervous relief passed through Nell Zoyland's perfect breasts, and through her ravished but unconceiving womb, and through her thighs and through her trembling knees" (135). Movement is that which passes through itself. In this passing there is no transfer. Yet Venus – love's planetary immanency – can effectuate a transfer *of* this passing-without-transfer. "Some mysterious vibration had *passed* between the girl and that white planet in the western sky" (138; emphasis added). There is a distance *between* the planet and the girl; but that which is passed over from the planet to the girl is precisely that which does not know any passing, any transfer. Love is the unpassed "X" whose unpassedness passes through itself ("nervous relief passed through Nell") – but also the un-passed "X" which is passed on from one point in the universe to another in the very act of cancelling the validity of the distance which makes such a pass possible. Thus Venus and girl are on the one hand opposite extremes in a spatial cosmos, on the other hand they are each other's immanent inclusions in a spaceless cosmos without distance, passing, transcendence, and transfer. What is transferred 'from' Venus to Nell is the sense of a life-movement which makes this very transfer redundant. The various heavenly bodies and deities of *A Glastonbury Romance* are in this way fraught with a devastating nonchalance, a sense of superfluity, waste, and pointless expenditure. Neither Nell nor the narrator *needs* the galaxy of suprahuman beings. Love itself does not need the 'planet' tracing the orbit of affectivity's ellipsis – does not need exteriority, circumference, space, horizon... world. Love does not need its ellipsis – yet in this life of ours, and in this particular artifact, the space of love's ellipsoid bonus is nevertheless granted as the magnificent superfluity which adds itself as nonsensically to the literary imagination as the Glastonbury Pageant adds itself to Christian revelation.

I am possibly saying, then, that in *A Glastonbury Romance* "the Planet of Love" (140) as an astrological entity is emblematically an addition of love to itself – and that this addition, as a platform for a 'transfer' suggesting motion, calls attention to a paradox in movement itself: the absence in it of any interval; in fact, of the slightest trace of the world. This sense of motion as auto-motion, and consequently of affectivity as auto-affectivity, is accentuated by the idea that Nell Zoyland is not really in love with anyone. "She's in love with Love" (137). To be in love with love is to be the open love-abyss in which the vanishing of the self materializes beforehand as the affective truth of a self lacking selfhood. This self lacking selfhood is the *amorous self*, Venus's reception of Venus. The miraculousness of love is the ongoing ellipsis of this receptivity in which love receives itself without the aid of any selfhood, personhood, identity, or reflection. Love is extraneous, planetary, 'astrological' precisely because its affectivity lacks the logic of the worldly mechanisms characterizing *life on Earth*. Love is not life on Earth – not even for earthly lovers like John and Mary Crow. For in love, in Glastonbury, in romance, Earth itself does not belong *to Earth*. In *A Glastonbury Romance*, Earth is not understood as Earth but as a planetary space crisscrossed by the sensation of affects that bypass the very media that make them possible. That which is 'passed' over to lovers 'from' planet Venus is the originary force which beforehand annuls all passing. To be touched by Venus is to loose the sense of the possibility of an interval between self and love and between love and itself – the very interval that love ought to require in the first place in order to perform the distant, long-range deed of its affective transit.

Now if movement in essence is not the closing of an interval, if on the contrary it is the sense of the absence of all intervals, the animal sensation of well-being that allows the beast to pass at each instant through the pure, transparent solidity of its own fluid flesh... then there can be no apprehension of any ontological difference between the sense of the flow of the light of "the great planet of the evening" and the "nervous relief" that "passe[s] through" love's breasts, womb, thighs, and knees (135). If movement, phenomenologically speaking, is not the closing of an interval, then a girl's "inordinate mania for romance" (139) is not different from the "wicked game" (127) played by those who consider that "idealism is puff-ball foolishness" (133). If romance *is movement*, and if the "wicked game" too *is movement* – then the affectivity of the one is by the same token the affectivity of the other – despite the two contrasting emotive realities. Here we are not dealing with reality, least of all with emotive reality. We are dealing instead with that which is manifested on this side of emotive reality. Movement is the affectivity that arises on this side of 'real' motion and on this side of emotive 'reality.' In *A Glastonbury Romance*, it is the felt, mobile animality which permits a father and an owl to be one and the same hoot. "That's my father; that's not an owl" (138). It is the felt, mobile animality that recognizes no originary, affective difference between the "shambling speed" of Sam Dekker (138) and the "idea of a wild otter caught in a trap" (137). It is the felt mobile animality that recognizes no originary, affective difference between "the swish of a horse's tail" and "a heifer's up-tossed head," between "the long relaxed shiver" of erotic excitement in a shapely girl and the phosphorescent Venus-light of the slow-flowing water on the banks of the stream that passes close to Whitelake Cottage (135). Heavenly bodies and deities are real in *A Glastonbury Romance* in so far as they are felt *by the animal-reader...* in other words by a reader who cognizes the 'doings' of the most far-fetched astro-physical being as the movement of a celestial 'animal' in itself... as the brutish 'passing' of movement through the living flesh of its own essence.

Movement has to do with the Mystery of Glastonbury as such – hence also with the Grail. It is important not to trivialize the animating complexity of this Mystery. It is foolish to reduce the affectivity of the Glastonbury Mystery to a simple interaction between 'sex' and 'religion.' Movement is more basic than either 'sex' or 'religion' – being the inert, originary motility that makes these two possible in the first place. This basic inertia-as-motility ensures the affinity between the non-ideal love-making of the Crow cousins (on the one hand) and the "essence" (125) of Glastonbury (on the other hand). John and Mary are deliberately foregrounded as "shamelessly devoid of any Ideal Love." "Their love was lust, a healthy, earthy, muddy, weather-washed lust, like the love of water-rats in Alder Dyke or the love of badgers on Brandon Heath"

(125). But when transferred from Norfolk to Glastonbury – a transfer which itself is an instantiation of movement – they come to stand in the atmospherium of movement *as such*, of the movement which lacks transfer and which for this reason is the quiver of an originary immobility. "And in the etheric atmosphere about these two, as they stood there" by a little gate in a privet-hedge in Glastonbury, "*quivered* the immemorial Mystery of Glastonbury" (125; emphasis added). The implication is that not only Mary and John but their actual lust comes to stand in the spot where movement, as quiver, lacks transfer. To be *transferred* from Norfolk to Glastonbury is on the one hand (1) to be transported from a secular, earthy part of England to an idealized, 'religious,' mythologized part of England. It is to leave a commonsensical domain in order to enter a region of undulating orchards and vaporous pastures – a region where blue-purple mists fluctuate in a space which is "the lowest pastoral country in the land of England, lower than the level of the sea" (121). But to be *transferred* from Norfolk to Glastonbury is on the other hand (2) to effectuate no relinquishing of the lust of primary movement whatsoever. The 'ideality' of the Glastonbury Mystery is no less movement-oriented than the earthy badger-existence of the lecherous cousins from East Anglia. 'Sex,' in order to be erotic, has to engage with the primary quiver, with movement *as such*. 'Glastonbury' is thus not a lessening of the erotic but a heightening of it, the confirmation of movement by itself in itself. The words used to suggest the 'idealizing' qualities of the low-lying West Country landscape – "fluctuating," "stirred," "vaporous," "undulating," etc – all suggest movement. The idea of a "[d]im and rich and vague" valley covered with "an undulating veil of blue-purple mist" produces the sense of perpetual movement through the image of the sea:... "lower than the level of the sea" (125). Glastonbury is sea-like – in the sense that here myths, dreams, superstitions, ideas, fantasies, hallucinations, reveries, obsessions and innumerable other affects sweep back and forth like the tides of a gigantic ocean bearing the incoherent but interfluid hopes and insanities of mankind. This sea-sick, rocking, mobile sensation – centred on the idea of the sea – is brought to consummation through the work's final staging of an all-encompassing flood... a flood which installs movement as the sense of the arrival of a mobility phenomenalizing itself as a transubstantiation of land into water rather than as a mere landward transportation of water from the

Bristol Channel. Here we must not prematurely think that what is shown is the swamping of the one by the many, that the flood betokens some sort of breaking-up of unity into diversity, of identity into difference. Such an interpretation underestimates the subtlety of the work's personality – a personality, I assert, which is profoundly concerned with the nature of movement *as such*. Movement *as such* is indifferent to the conventionalized debates in the academies about the possible pre-eminence of identity over difference or of difference over identity. The tiresome arguments about the One and the Many, Unity and Plurality, Presence and Otherness are all metaphysical. Movement (the flood) is not. The flood *floods* these pseudo-controversies... as does movement itself. What movement turns its attention to in *A Glastonbury Romance* *is movement*.

The narrator can create a complete lack of hostility between the Crow cousins and the Glastonbury Mystery (between East Anglia and the West Country) by making us feel that if movement in each of the two separate domains is movement *as such*, then movement in one domain *is* by the same token movement in the other. The animal-movement of cousins behaving like love-sick badgers and water-rats is no different, *qua* movement, from the movement in which the Glastonbury Mystery "quivered" (125). In each case, movement is in essence that which arises in itself, by itself. Indeed, movement is in each case that which arises as *caused* by itself. In a trivial sense, the Mystery is a product of semiosis – each creature finding a significance in it, or giving it one. But on a deeper level, the Mystery is untouched by semiosis, by interpretation, by hermeneutics. "[A]s different people approached it they changed its chemistry, *though not its essence*" (125; emphasis added). The Glastonbury Mystery never produces "the same psychic effect" (125); but on the level where we disregard effects, we regard the essence of the Mystery itself, in other words movement. The Glastonbury Mystery is movement; but so is the "weather-washed lust" (125) of John and Mary Crow. "Mary seized his wrist with all her fingers and *lifted* it to her mouth... 'It smells like peat,' she thought, and she began licking with the tip of her tongue the little hairs which now tickled her lips. This gave her a sharp tingling sensation that *ran through her whole frame*. In a flash she imagined herself stretched out in bed by John's side" (124; emphasis added). Here I am not calling attention to the banal fact that love is typically accompanied by physical movements that are subject to empirical verification. Rather, I am calling attention to the narrator's way of foregrounding movement – a foregrounding that aims firstly to dig into the very nature of movement as such, and secondly to display its seamless vanishing into the life it initially seems to contradict – the movement of the Mystery. This contradiction between Mystery and "weather-washed lust" is cancelled – not only be the sense that the Mystery too is in full enjoyment of an ownmost, primal motility ("pouring *into*"; "sucked their life-blood *from*," 125; emphasis added) – but also by the sense that even the weather-washed love-making of lusty East Anglians is secretly based on the mystical instantaneity of fantasy, mind, imagination, hallucination, dream, wishful thinking, and magic transfer without transportation. The act in which Mary lifts John's fingers is quasi-religious, not merely 'physical.' The act in which she discovers that it smells of peat is more than material – being a ritualizing in the flesh of the powers of auto-revelation given to the self by itself. The act in which the "tingling sensation... ran through her whole frame" annuls all sense of a mind/ body split – "whole frame" implying a totality that cares little for such academic distinctions. And finally the fact that she "imagined" herself in bed with her lover "[i]n a flash" points to the lack of separation between flesh and flash... between the body and the revelation of the body to the mind, between the revelation of the body to itself through the body and the revelation of the body to itself through the mind, between the revelation of the body through the body and the revelation of the body through revelation, between the revelation of revelation through flesh and the revelation of revelation through revelation.

This last-mentioned possibility – which from a 'logical' viewpoint is strictly speaking nonsensical – is the stuff and fabric of *A Glastonbury Romance*... and ultimately indeed of art, thought, meditation, reading, religion. That the medium 'through' which revelation is revealed happens to be revelation itself – this is the prime mystery of life, indeed of revelation. In *A Glastonbury Romance* it undermines from the outset the proud notion of a First Cause, displayed on the work's first page. For the narrator does not simply inform us that the influence of the Glastonbury Mystery "had its... origin in the nature of the Good-Evil First Cause"; he asserts that this Mystery-influence "had its own *sui generis* origin in the nature of the Good-Evil First Cause" (125). To succumb beforehand to the *sui generis* principle is to succumb to the principle establishing an entity as its own origin. This idea that an entity is its own origin applies *a fortiori* to the origin itself – in theology thus to God. The origin is not merely an origin. What sets apart an origin from all other beings is not the fact that it is a first cause but on the contrary the fact that it is its own cause, that it *causes itself*. This is the clue to the principle of movement. In *A Glastonbury Romance* movement causes itself. In an important sense this too is what the work of art does. It is generated by its own being, animated by its own life. There is a suggestion of defiance in such a conception – which is why commentators who quickly smooth-over the *sui generis* principle as some sort of easily-understood ontotheological notion forwarded by tradition prematurely run ahead of themselves... and progressively into more and more inconsequential 'readings' of the artifact.

To say that movement, as a *sui generis* event, is a clue to the work is not to say that movement is a master-key, a god. For the paradox is that the *sui generis* principle, *applied equally to all beings*, gives to each creature an absolute autonomy from all others – even, in a way, from the First Cause. This applies to the Glastonbury Mystery itself – so that in this work the emphasis is not really on Mystery but on Glastonbury. The Mystery-influence "had its own *sui generis* origin in the nature of the Good-Evil First Cause, but it had grown to be more and more an independent entity as the centuries rolled over it" (125). I am saying, then, that the Glastonbury Mystery is an origin – a "Fount of Life," or "Secret Thing" (126) – that affects itself. This self-affecting is the principle of life – indeed it is life itself. In phenomenology, the technical-philosophic name for this self-affecting is 'auto-affection' or 'auto-affectivity.' Its name in the present essay *is movement*. From the current perspective, then, so-called desire (sex, lust, possessive craving, the idealizing event of being in love with love itself) is nothing less than movement... and movement is that which passes through itself, that which affects itself. The great Hegel touched this idea when he spoke of desire [*Begierde*] as something that desired itself. But in his greatness Hegel made the familiar Western mistake of installing *the interval* between the phenomenon and itself. When he famously spoke of 'desire for desire,' he installed *the interval* between desire and itself – so that desire, in coming to desire itself, makes a loop through the world before it returns to the point in its orbit from which it departed. However, life posits no such loop, distance, orbit, interval, difference, or hiatus between itself and itself. *Movement* does not need any space, any distance-from-self to be that which it is, *viz.*, movement. As *movement*, in other words as origin, will, desire, and feeling, the Mystery of Glastonbury does not need any exterior realm of semiotic or representational visibility to be what it is. The Holy Grail does not require a tablet, an exterior 'writing-space'... in order to be. For its mode of manifestation (movement!) is not a mode of inscription in the first place. The Grail is not written... or strictly speaking even perceived. It is felt. Feelings are not inscribed. They do not even 'appear.' They simply move in movement itself – and *are* this auto-affecting of movement by itself. One is not surprised, then, to learn that the "muddy" (125) lust of the Crow cousins is a desire which is "urged by its own intensity" (126). Nor is one surprised to learn that this *sui generis* desire, "rooted in fen-mud and vicious heathenism," is "caught up" by the "desires of two thousand years, which in that valley had *pulsed* and *jetted* and *spouted*" (126; emphasis added). Because it is movement, and because movement is auto-affectivity, the "brutish and carnal purpose" of East Anglian lust is indifferently also all other forms of self-affection... including the letting-itself-be-affected-by-itself known as the Glastonbury Mystery. There is strictly speaking no 'reciprocation' of desire 'between' John and Mary – for even this idea of reciprocation trivializes the event itself, *viz.*, movement. Nor is there really some sort of ongoing reciprocation between lust and Grail, between East Anglia and the West Country. In so far as they are movement, each is the other... absolutely. Movement, that which pulses, jets, and spouts, in the final analysis pulses, jets, and spouts in itself. There is a pulsation of movement in itself: this is desire... but also the Grail. There is a jetting of movement in itself: this is love... but also the Grail. There is a spouting of movement in and through itself: this is pure lust... but also the Mystery. The Glastonbury Mystery is not static. It is a "Numen" which is "wind-blown" (126). To approach it is to be in the gathering electricity and "atomic air" (126) where it approaches *itself.* The approaching-itself of the Mystery, of the Grail – indeed of desire – is invisible... but so is movement, so is the Grail, so is life itself. No one has 'seen' life. No one has 'seen' the Grail. What is 'seen' is rather vision itself. Movement does not have eyes – but it is in essence visionary.

To be "shamelessly devoid of any Ideal Love" (125) is not to prefer the visible over the invisible – any more than the act of dwelling in the vicinity of the Mystery is to live in a site where movement is personal rather than impersonal, material rather than immaterial, existential rather than essential. Since movement – life's originary urge to desire and affect *itself* – is not in the world but on this side of the world, it is also on this side of the binary oppositions which construct 'the world,' and which conceal the Mystery that makes the world possible *as life* in the first place. The Mystery-influence "was personal and yet impersonal, it was a material centre of force and yet an immaterial fountain of life" (125).

I am emphasizing, then, the manner in which Glastonbury is understood as movement. Glastonbury moves into itself... because the Mystery moves into itself – being in the final analysis nothing but this self-movement by movement in itself. Movement's auto-affection, its 'love' of its own life, is life's own 'love' of its own life. Life is always life loving life *as movement.* In this 'love' – which Schopenhauer called will [*Wille*] – there is always a sense of free activity... yet at the same time a sense of closure. For there is no way in which life, in the living capacity of its own ongoing nature, can refuse to be... life. Life is *compelled* to be that which it is, to move within the scope of its own movement. In a sense, therefore, movement actually goes nowhere; movement takes us nowhere; movement *moves* nowhere. 'We' travel. Our 'existence' travels. But life itself does not. I may move from Bristol to New York – but in this transfer, life itself (movement) never moves outside its own boundary (movement). Movement as such is never properly speaking transferred, never shifted out and away into an exterior space. Life, *qua* life, never escapes from its own domain. This sense that life is at once movement and movement's lack of transfer, this sense that movement is motion as living inertia, comes alive in the impact made on the human mind by *stone*. To receive the impact of the event of beholding *stone* is by no means the mere act of recognizing a solid mass of 'matter' as inertia. For the secret of each sincere apperception of stone is that this apperception is shaped not only by an originary sense of the power of inertia but also by an originary sense of movement... by a sense of inertia as movement... by a sense of the inertia that movement in the final analysis is. Movement (in other words life) is 'inert' for the simple reason that it is doomed to remain in the indestructible shell of its own essence. What is this essence? It is – *to live*! Life is thus not simply a fact, or 'experience' – but, as it were, a command. Stone is a peculiarly forthright instantiation of this command – and imposes itself upon man as it imposes itself on itself. The 'command' of stone is not dictatorial, however – but is, as Magritte has shown, a free-floating defiance. The 'nonchalance' of stone equals its imperative need to be purely that which it is, to stand in the outline of its own formal destiny.

Now in Chapter 3, 'Stonehenge,' John Cowper shows his keen awareness of these mineralogical implications. Stone is a closure, whether it is a henge or not. But movement's indwelling inertia, expressed so readily in stone as the indwelling inertia of life, inheres not only in the mineral but also in the human being. Those persons who attain Mystery-significance in Glastonbury are those individuals who most clearly exhibit the originary inertia of life – the appearing-act in which movement appears 'to' itself only. There is "something pathetically animal-like" about Sam Dekker (115). He is often seen standing "in a heavy daze" (115). He takes it for granted that he is too unpractical and cowardly to elope with Nell Zoyland (116). His very passion is a matter of inertia. "All he could do was to go on constantly seeing her." He views himself as that which in a sense he really is: "an ugly, lumpish, uninteresting failure" (116). Nell's reckless love for him is from this viewpoint nothing less than a love for life itself – a love for 'movement' as that which is fatally stuck in its own 'lump.' Sam's love for trees is much the same – the tree being a species of petrified vegetation, of 'growth' locked in the inertia it secretly is. For his rival, William Zoyland, Sam is a "frail seedling-shoot" that needs to be nipped in the bud (118); but for the narrator and for the reader Sam is a being who is not altogether different from the immemorial oak tree whose corrugated torso becomes the life-body sought by his soul as he bows forward towards it, his outstretched arms extended in 'stupid' devotion. Sam's 'stupidity' is the stupidity of the Grail, of Glastonbury... of life. This stupidity belongs to movement as such – and the purer movement is (the closer it stays to its own essential nature), the more 'stupid' it is. This stupidity catches the eye of the work's imaginative passion – so that in the 'stupid' movements of Crummy Geard's dazed body-vanity there is no less truth than in the Grail itself; so that in the 'stupid' movements of her sister Cordelia's body-coldness there is a clandestine display of a secret at the very heart of life – a secret that 'moves'...

but which in this very mobilization of itself effectuates no departure, embarkation, or transcendence. To descend to "the verdurous island of Avalon" (129) is to effectuate a descent from existence to life, from movement as travel to movement as inertia, stone, blood, Grail, water, punishment, ecstasy, and pain.

It is from this viewpoint that the entire idea of turning Glastonbury into a site intended for mass-pilgrimage is not only ecologically preposterous but ontologically bizarre. This is not to say that travel and life-as-inertia are mutually exclusive; for when we are told that Elizabethans and men in cavalier ringlets have touched the indented bark of the massive oak embraced by Sam Dekker "with their travel-swollen bare hands" (129), the word 'travel-swollen' moves within itself to give a sense of travel as an inertia whose movement is flesh swelling to the limits of life yet never dreaming of overstepping these limits. Travelling is here compatible with life as inertia, and with inertia as 'movement.' No such compatibility is at hand when Owen Evans speaks of Mr. Geard's vision of bringing "shoals and shoals of pilgrims" to Glastonbury – "from France, from Germany, from Russia" (159). Somehow these "pilgrims" do not seem – even in theory – capable of making the kind of journey to Glastonbury effectuated by John Crow via Stonehenge. We can see these "pilgrims" in front of us, forming a huge system of mystic "influence" (159), in other words inflow. But movement, as the inertia that allows life to fluidly affect itself, is something other than "influence." Movement, as originary inertia, cannot be a simple coming-to-Glastonbury. This is why John Cowper does not show us a man called John Crow travelling toward Glastonbury. Although John Crow 'travels,' it is not the fact that he travels that phenomenalizes him as movement. What phenomenalizes John Crow as movement... is John himself, his very nature – which, as it happens, is life, affectivity affecting affectivity *on this side* of the world.

Accordingly, in reading the opening chapters of *A Glastonbury Romance*, one needs to sensitize oneself to the way in which the narrator allows us to become acquainted with each significant character *through movement* – in other words through the originary inertia that wells up in the living being as the life *of* this being *in* and *as* movement. To become acquainted with John Crow is to become acquainted with "the hereditary twitch in his face" (158). To become acquainted with Mr. Geard is to become acquainted with the peculiar movement of "his hydrocephalic head" as it swings "on the pivot of his neck with the slow gravity of the ghost in Punch and Judy" (157). These remarks are not Dickensian; they are not manufactured in order to refine a portrait of a living entity inhabiting a world, or even to adumbrate the world-forces that may be the secret underpinning of such a world. On the contrary, such remarks pertain to the business of opening the question of movement (i.e. life) *as such*. They probe into the ways in which movement 'travels' into movement – this interior travelling being no 'inner' journey into the soul but a true following of movement itself as it dives inwardly through its own inertia during the course of life's astonishing sensation of itself. In Sam, in John, and in a variety of other significant characters, this auto-affection has an animal quality. But if Sam Dekker is an animal, if John Crow is an animal – this is not so because the narrator is interested in some zoological 'reality' that may (or may not) be the 'material' base of life. The animal quality of a Dekker or a Crow or a Zoyland or a Geard is not 'biological.' Life here does not mean *bios*, life-of-the-organism. Life means *life* – the inert event of being trapped in the movement we happen to be living in. Although "[t]he idea of a wild otter caught in a trap" is obnoxious to Sam Dekker (137), life *as movement* is in a special sense (much exploited by Powys) this very animal sense of being trapped. *Movement is always trapped in movement* – and no movement has ever managed to extricate itself from 'movement' in general and as such. The otter, the stone, the lover – these are all trapped... not in themselves, not in 'life' (if by this we mean 'existence,' biological self-presence), but in the inertia that cannot be explained and whose movement the work will come to hallucinate as the Grail.

Crummie and Cordelia Geard too are trapped. This closure which life effectuates in each of them as the motility of the inertia of life slipping through itself phenomenalizes itself as the *small movements made by Crummie* and as the *small movements made by Cordelia*. We first see Crummie lying in bed on her back. Her hair is fair, her eyes violet-coloured, her skirts rumpled. There is a show of white skin between her stockings and her drawers; her slippers are "kicking peevishly" in a mood of "sleepy petulance" (152). In this coquettish frame of mind, Crummie toys with her skirt and begins "caressing, with the conscious narcissism of a girl inordinately proud of her legs, the soft flesh above one of her knees." We are then progressively given further glimpses of Crummie as auto-affection. We see her move the softness of her hand away "from her satiny flesh" as she pulls down her skirt (153). We see her pull up her legs under her "with the complete abandonment of a very little girl" (154). We see her bend her head so that the waves of her hair fall "in loose wisps and loops" on her lap (154). We see her swing her legs off the bed; we see her "clutching tight in her fingers the midstream of her mass of fragrant hair, pulling it round her white neck and passing the comb, with many cries at the tangles, through its down-shaken wavy curls" (155). She proceeds to twist the loveliness of her hair round her head, stick hairpins into it. She slips off her dress, bends over a chest of drawers, and looks "leisurely for this and that other garment; weighing, rejecting, appraising, selecting. Hovering there, all in white, with bare arms and bare shoulders, she proceeded to smooth down with indolent outspread fingers the creases of her slip, preparatory to pulling her dress over her head" (155). The movement-words utilized for the purpose of displaying Crummie as auto-affection – "caressing" (152), "pulled," "bent," "covering," (154), "swung," "clutching," "pulling," "passing," "twist," "stick," "slipped off," "smooth down" (155) – are ostensibly given as clues to her personality, supposedly one that is given to "narcissism" (152). In actual fact, however, the movement-words have an infinitely more profound directedness... being clues not to Crummie but to life. For what we are shown when we are shown Crummie's movements *is life*. Life is thus not what lies 'behind" movements, what movements supposedly 'point' to. Life *is these movements*. This does not mean that life is in essence 'physical,' that life's reality is the choreography of its material hazards as expressed in bodily movements. It means that life is constantly showing itself *to itself* in the manifestation of movement moving freely through the apparent purposelessness of its own secret inertia. The notion that movement in Powys points to 'sensuality' (in the ordinary sense) crumbles as soon as we realize that movement as auto-affection is just as evident in a 'non-sensual,' plain girl like Cordelia as in her supposedly more sensual sister. Auto-affection is most evident not when the narrator permits us to enjoy the fairly-standardized views of Crummie's natural sensuality but in the more fragile (because less self-conscious) movements of her sister.

> Cordelia moved now to the table and began folding up her embroidery.
> 'I must go down and put on my coral necklace,' she said to herself, 'and brush my hair a bit; but what's the use? If he [Owen Evans] doesn't like me for myself, he won't care. And if he does he won't care either!' And then the queer thought came into her head – 'If a man wants to marry a girl, when he likes her *for her mind alone*, does he get *any* pleasure from kissing her and embracing her?' So deep did this queer and troubling question sink into her consciousness that she let her embroidery lie where it fell, unwrapt in its usual piece of blue tissue paper! She herself sank down on her sewing-chair and stared in front of her. She stared at the particular one of the pictures of 'The Four Seasons' which represented Autumn. Quite automatically she read: 'We *too* have Autumns, when our leaves fall loosely through the misty air, and all our good is bound in sheaves, and we stand reaped and bare.' She had read these words in their familiar place on the wall of the sewing-room since she could read at all. (155)

Like the 'Four Seasons' picture, the narrator is saying something about life. But whereas the discourse of the picture is metaphysical, the narrator's is not. The narrator does not make any existential claims about life, or about the supposed relations between life, sentiment, and self. For that which life is is not revealed by what we feel, or by the rapport between self-feeling and the world... but by movement itself as we feel the helpless inertia of our joys and dilemmas. The thrills and sorrows of existence are not themselves life. Their resolution, non-resolution, consummation, or default is a matter of indifference to life. But what is not a matter of indifference to life is the motion in which Cordelia's queer question comes to "sink into her consciousness." This sinking, *as sinking*, is movement as such... in other words life. Life is indifferent to the question of whether Evans gets any pleasure from embracing Cordelia; life is indeed indifferent even to the matter of whether Evans loves her for her mind alone or not. But what life is not indifferent to is the manner in which Cordelia lets her embroidery lie where it fell, the manner in which *the sinking of movement into itself* becomes the motion of a plain sister who "sank down on her sewing-chair and stared in front of her" (155). Life is not indifferent to the way in which Cordelia's eyes sink into the picture-and-words on the wall – for this typical, aboriginary sinking... expressing a 'reading' that occurs prior to semiosis and interpretation... is the illiterate 'fall' of movement (Cordelia) into itself as it occurs at the beginning of life – in this beginning which always starts all over again, and whose event is movement moving in movement. *Life is never indifferent to life.*

Cordelia reads "[q]uite automatically" (155). This 'automatic reading,' far from being a weary loss of the focus of semiosis and of concentration – is the 'reading' that makes reading possible in the first place, the 'stupid' reading which we first direct toward reading-material so and so many months or years before we 'learn to read.' As a child Cordelia once came to a point where reading (in the empirical, semiotic sense) became possible. "She had read these words in their familiar place on the wall of the sewing-room *since she could read at all*" (155; emphasis added). But there is of course a point that antecedes the point where reading becomes possible. And I am asserting that this anterior point too is readerly – that this point anterior to reading is the readerly point *par excellence*. There is a readerly point prior to reading – and in the act of reading we always carry this point with us. There is an absence of reading in all reading... and it is this absence – *viz.*, life – which makes reading, literature, and the work possible in the first place. There is an absence of reading in all reading. For Cordelia, for the one who happens to be reading this very page of *A Glastonbury Romance*, the unspoken, unthought, and unimagined name of this absence is Imagination. Imagination precedes reading – not because we 'imagine' before we read, or because we are 'imaginatively' directed toward the 'reading' of our own bodies, but because reading, that which in essence is not semiotic, is movement. For Cordelia, the sinking-into-the-Four-Seasons-picture *and this picture itself* are indistinguishable. The sinking and the picture are conjointly (but without 'fusion') the movement that life is. The unit "since she could read at all" does not point to an anterior line of demarcation, a boundary in the past beyond which the pastward traveller could not move as readerly life. The unit "since she could read at all" points instead to an absolute beginning which, without ever having to effectuate a 'start,' always begins again.

Movement as auto-affection is not narcissism. Nor is it sensuality. On the contrary, movement as auto-affection *is life*. Auto-affection is not the self's affection for itself. It is not even life's affection for itself. It is life in general and as such. This is why there is 'hope' for an unattractive and exceedingly plain creature like Cordelia Geard. There is hope for Cordelia not because she can sensually, intellectually, or emotionally enjoy her own sweet life despite being physically unpleasing. There is hope for Cordelia *because life is feeling*.

Cordelia is thus mistaken in the very event of feeling pangs of envy *vis-à-vis* her far more beautiful sister – failing to recognize that this very envy is feeling... and that *in the suffering that feeling is...* life is fully around us and in us as life's certainty of its own tangible essence. In deprivation, then, we are never deprived of life – deprivation being this very life we feel we are deprived of. Cordelia's attempts to rationalize auto-affectivity fail for the simple reason that she intellectualizes self-affection – understanding it commonsensically as the self-reflection of the body, or of the æsthetic self.

> If God had willed everything from the very Beginning of the World, why had He willed that all this exquisite delight in one's own body... should be given to one girl, while another girl felt her body to be a troublesome burden to be carried about? Oh, it didn't depend on having men to admire one, or to embrace one. 'It is the feeling,' thought poor Cordelia, 'of being beautiful to one's own self that matters!' (156).

Cordelia here takes two significant steps, but fails to take the third. She has understood that auto-affection does not depend on the admiration of men. She has understood that auto-affection does not depend on the physical love-making of men. But she has not understood that auto-affection does not even depend on the distant or caressing love of *the self* either. Auto-affection has nothing whatsoever to do with the self. *It has to do with affection only.* *Affection* has to do with affection only. That there can be affection without self... this is incomprehensible to the self. But it is by no means incomprehensible to life, to affection. The 'story' of *A Glastonbury Romance* is in this way the 'story' of the Holy Grail... indeed of any profoundly religious life-tale – it is the 'story' of the discovery of life itself as the affective domain that does not need any 'self' or any other-worldly construct to be that which it is. But what is life then? It is movement-without-self... the act of loving and suffering without being 'someone' or 'something' effectuating this loving, effectuating this suffering. In life, life itself suffers – not the self. In life, love itself loves, not the self.

Does the narrator bring such a truth into view? He certainly does – and he does so throughout the work. In the present scene, he does so by shifting our regard from the inadequate *conceptualization* of auto-affection effectuated by Cordelia to an actual *revelation* of auto-affection inadvertently effectuated by Crummie. This revelation has a readerly-semiotic appearance but is itself not readerly-semiotic. It is a small sketch made on a card stuck in the edge of a picture-frame. It is a self-portrait *without self*... a self-portrait bearing the inscription "Crummie *by* Crummie, Aged Six" (156). This sketch is so infantile, crude, and smudged that is cannot be viewed as a proper portrait. What is 'depicted' is not a self, not a being, but that which has not yet acquired the firm, adult outlines of representational thinking. "Crummie by Crummie" does not belong to the world – the 'by' (in "Crummie by Crummie") being too weak, slender, and undeveloped to be viewed as a fully-reflexive go-between between a self and itself. The 'Crummie' that is (not) depicted belongs to art *as such* rather than to art – just as the artifacts of the Aborigine belong to painting *as such* rather than to the 'history of painting.' "Crummie by Crummie" belongs to a space (life itself) where the world has not yet formed – to the shapeless realm on this side of the world where that which has true shape is in essence the invisible only... feeling, movement, suffering, revelation. Instead of changing her clothes and making herself more attractive in front of the mirror, Cordelia merely pats her hair, shakes her skirt, and removes some threads from its surface.

> Instead of glancing at the mirror, she glanced, over her sister's head, at the coloured representation of Spring, the first of those Four Seasons, hanging on the wall. At the bottom of this picture, which had always been the younger's favourite of all four, was a little card, stuck in the edge of the frame, carrying on its surface a childish sketch of a small girl, done in crude pinks and blues, the hair just an enormous smudge of chrome-yellow, which bore the inscription 'Crummie by Crummie, Aged Six.' (156)

The childish sketch is not inserted in *A Glastonbury Romance* as a *representation* of auto-affection. For auto-affection is precisely that which cannot be represented – in other words exemplified, illustrated, placed before the regard of the intentional eye. What makes auto-affectivity real in *A Glastonbury Romance* is not an image of 'it' but movement as such. The reader is not asked to contemplate "Crummie by Crummie, Aged Six" as an instantiation of auto-affection. Indeed it is utterly unlikely that the reader will pause at this juncture and *think* anything at all. What makes "Crummie by Crummie" auto-affectively poignant is instead the work's ongoing preoccupation with movement as such – in this case with the furtive way in which Cordelia gives her hair certain "pats," with the way in which she gives her skirt a certain "shake," and with the way in which she "picked off the front of it a few coloured threads left by her embroidery" (156). It is the myriads of references to such furtive movements that make up the bulk of the comprehensive affectivity of *A Glastonbury Romance* – in the manner that the bulk of an Atlantic whale is made up of the plankton it constantly eats. Movement in *A Glastonbury Romance* is planktonic. Planktos means 'drifting,' from the Greek *plazesthai*, to wander, drift, pass. The work is the movement it invisibly digests, the assimilation of its own movement through movement. But the movement, being the work, is also that which consumes itself – being the loose drifting of a movement that loses itself without expenditure in its inhering lack of trajectory. As I have asserted, there is a flotation of originary inertia in such a mystical conception of life – affectivity being the weakly-swimming, passively-floating body of movement that causes life to vanish in the act of its self-feeling.

Once inertia is understood as movement, origin, and auto-affectivity, it becomes obvious that the narrator's characterization of woman as a creature who is in touch with the sense of "the universal prostitute" (139) is not a sexist commentary on the 'lowness' of women – but a commentary that looks at such a cliché through irony. The "physical passivity which women have the power of summoning up, to endure the inconvenience of an amorous excitement which they do not share" (139), is not a passivity betokening the subserviency of females to males. This is why the "imaginative pity" directed at women by sentimental, idealizing men who are less thick-skinned than the male sadists who cunningly believe themselves to be exploiting this "passivity" is no more lucid than the unfeeling assault of erotic violence itself. The sentimental male and the thick-skinned male both believe that passivity is passivity – that the supposed lack of 'enjoyment,' because it is an empirical lack, is real. "When a man sees a sensitive girl with what he considers a thick-skinned, brutal male, he experiences a twinge – perhaps quite uncalled for – of the sort of imaginative pity which is the inverse side of male sadism" (139). It is important not to make a thick-skinned reading of Powys here – one which, in following the stereotypical rationale of political correctness, urges us to review the narrator as a male chauvinist locked in 'prejudices' about sex, femininity, and power. Such a reading would need to forget the inverted commas heralding the expression "the universal prostitute," and to forget the word 'perhaps' in "perhaps quite uncalled for" (139). Clearly there are innumerable cases where the imaginative pity of the empathizing sensitive male is legitimate and welcome. But what the narrator is discussing is not these cases – but those altogether different and no less common ones where it is the rude insensitivity of man that prompts the deeper commitments of Venus. Which commitments? The commitments of Venus *to herself*. It is this commitment of Venus to herself, auto-affectivity, which is Powys's main topic of amorous interest in *A Glastonbury Romance*. Accordingly, it is naive to assert that all the various forms of erotic excitement felt by a woman in the presence of a man who fails to provide direct body-to-body sex-enjoyment are in essence masochistic. For it belongs to the nature of Venus to love not simply beings and bodies but love itself – or, more precisely, love as something affecting itself. A woman can love a man who is not currently 'giving her pleasure,' if she feels that she is in command of the secret of auto-affectivity as such. "Few men realize the depth of the satisfaction to women's nature in the mere possession of the power to cause such excitement" (139). The expression "women's nature," taken out of the context of the novel's delineation of auto-affectivity, is in essence sexist. But this expression is not an abstract proposition submitted to the general public in a debating hall. It is situated in a work which perpetually delves into the nature of Venus by delving into the nature of movement. The expression "women's nature," once seen in its fictional-discursive context, is indistinghishable from the name Venus. The Greek equivalent, *Aphrodite*, occurs on this selfsame page (139). To be Venus means: to hold sway over the field in which affectivity appears as auto-affectivity, as love affecting *itself*. This field... *is life*. The threat of Venus, then, is in fact the *threat of life* – the threat that Sam comes to know when Nell appeals to those very thick-skinned qualities *in him* which he fails to understand as the clues to the 'madness' of the act of ravishing. "Why didn't you just carry me off, Sam dearest, that evening on Queen's Sedgemoor? We'd have managed somehow. I'm not a fool; and you've got such strong arms!" (167).

Movement now occurs in Sam as something that moves in itself. "Sam drew a deep breath; so deep that it shook him from head to foot. He felt a leap in the pit of his stomach, as if a fish had risen there" (167). Venus clinches the matter by informing Sam that she has been ravished by her most thick-skinned love-partner in the crudest possible fashion.

> 'It is too late *now*, my dearest,' she said.
> 'Why is it?' he groaned.
> 'Because... because he's made me give myself to him... as I've never done... before this.'
> Sam was silent, pondering in his brain the inscrutable twists and turns of women's hearts. He thought to himself, 'What am I to believe? That day we went to Pomparlès Bridge and looked at the dace in those pools, and she told me about Arthur's sword, she made me believe he had ravished her the first day they met; and now she says this!" (168).

Contrary to what he thinks, what Sam has become entangled in is neither Nell nor 'woman' – but Venus. It is thus pointless to ask an existential, behaviourist question like, "Do women delight to make themselves out victims?" (168) – for what is at stake in *A Glastonbury Romance*, as indeed in life, is not the interactivity of desires, schemes, and forces... but the manifestation of the field where movement surges in itself as movement. Venus moves in Venus as Nell moves in Nell. Sam will in the long run most certainly become sexually excited by the idea that Nell herself is as secretly thick-skinned as her husband-ravisher. But this person-to-person excitement is of no consequence to Venus itself – for affectivity moves in itself whether feeling is jealous or serene, thick-skinned or thin-skinned. The clue to 'Nell' is in this way not her discursive and erotic shiftiness but the movements that movement *itself* makes in and for her... in an aura that stands round her flesh as something almost beyond her ken. It is within this carnal halo that we see her "draw her hand up and down the polished edge of the seat" in the church where they secretly meet (168). It is within this carnal halo that we perceive her "moving her feet a little, as if the ground was slippery beneath her" – that we see her "poking the end of her umbrella into a crevice between two stones" (167). It is within this carnal halo, too, that we see Venus as a goddess who is illuminated not by the pleasure that an extraneous creature may 'give' her but by the pleasure that no one can give – the event of auto-affectivity as a pleasure that affects itself... and as something that becomes *pleasant* precisely in so far as it is allowed to stand clearly in the truth of this self-affecting. Venus is the goddess of love *because* she does not need any being exterior to her own presence in order to *be love*. The 'passivity' of Venus is thus not an act in which she 'sacrifices' her own capacity for self-enjoyment in order to let 'someone else' enjoy himself at her expense; the 'passivity' of Venus is her indifference to auto-affection's specific locus. For her there is as much excitement in the auto-affectivity that occurs in a realm that 'transcends' her own as there is in the auto-affectivity that occurs in a realm that is immanent to herself. Why? Because an auto-affectivity that 'transcends' Venus secretly always remains, *qua auto-affection*, non-transcending, immanent. The love that 'transcends' Venus remains immanent to Venus – Venus herself being this love in the first place.

Venus is thus the planet whose halo is herself. She is the goddess whose love-ray never overshoots the edge of her own disc. Such an order of things makes no sense to a rationalist like Red Robinson, the materialist man of political revolution who sees any stellar system as "useful" in so far as it "afforded light" (175). He knows less than the narrator about the bodies and motions that do not belong to the world "– was it Cassiopeia? Red Robinson was weak on the subject of stars" (175). He is not likely to realize that the life he lives is ultimately not governed by history or politics but by movement as such – as that which, like Venus, moves in the irradiating feeling of its own life. This movement of movement in itself – in other words life – weighs heavily on some creatures, as is demonstrated by the tormented existence of Owen Evans. For creatures like John and Mary Crow this selfsame auto-affection is no burden – but rather a nothing, a sport, a picnic. For Glastonbury it is a mystery in matter – a mystery that communicates itself to the reader as the sense of being trapped in the very pastoral nature which the work patiently outlines as a perpetual transcendence-within-immanence... as the ongoing sense that life, that indeed Glastonbury itself, never 'leaves' its own secret... but rotates in it. Accordingly, we follow Sam Dekker much as Sam Dekker follows William Zoyland: with a sense that the presence of smells, of animals, of sounds, and of thoughts is an acceptance of a strange reality of life in presence itself, in the Parousia that even the author himself could not fathom.

> After following a kind of tow-path along the bank they came to a small river weir. There was a gurgling sound under the woodwork here, and a low humming and rustling sound; both sounds were evidently being caused by the position of the dam at that hour, but it was too dark to distinguish them exactly.

Out of the darkness of that full-brimmed swishing water there emerged a damp, chilly, but not unpleasant smell, composed of wet moss, of old dead leaves, of yet older dead wood, of long-submerged, slime-coated masonry, of clammy river weeds. The gurgling sound and the rushing sound came forth hollowly together, producing upon the ear a kindred effect to that produced upon the sense of smell by the damp wafture. (137)

A Glastonbury Romance would be pointless without descriptions such as these. They are in essence not descriptive but affective. They are animated by a sense of animal presence – indeed of animal entrapment – which in the current episode becomes the concrete fear of a trapped otter, and which in the experience of seriously re-reading the work becomes the somewhat unsettling sense of actually being physically caught in the artifact's reality. This sensation, which is unmistakably the sensation also of *Hamlet, Lear, David Copperfield, Wuthering Heights*, and other works of immemorial hypnosis, is the sensation of life itself... of life as something which, if we are free and courageous, is that which is affected only by itself.

Primary Source

Powys, John Cowper. *A Glastonbury Romance*. London: Picador, 1975; 1933.

Secondary Sources

Henry, Michel. *C'est moi la vérité: pour une philosophie du christianisme*. Paris: Seuil, 1996.
—. *Phénoménologie matérielle*. Paris: Presses universitaires de France, 1990.
Schopenhauer, Arthur. *The World as Will and Representation*. Translated by E. F. J. Payne, Volume 1. New York: Dover Publications, 1969; 1819.

IAN HUGHES
The Genre of John Cowper Powys's Major Novels

One of the factors underlying the mixed critical response to John Cowper Powys's prose fiction has been a confusion about its formal nature – that is, its genre. Powys, I am sure, had a clear idea of what he was trying to do. He did not always succeed, but at least he knew that he was trying to write 'philosophic romance'.

If we can come to understand better what sort of creature a philosophic romance is, we may be in a better position to evaluate Powys's success and failure as a novelist. It comes down to horses for courses. We do not normally criticise the domestic cat because it does not bark or wag its tail when pleased, or the domestic dog because it does not purr or have retractable claws. It would seem just as pointless to claim that, say, *Tristram Shandy* is a better novel than *Middlemarch* as that *King Lear* is a better poem than *Paradise Lost*. Similarly, if Powys's best philosophic romances are good philosophic romances, it seems absurd to claim that, say, *The Heart of the Matter* is a better novel than *Wolf Solent*.

The seminal influence on Powys's understanding of philosophic romance is the work of Walter Pater, and the master-key to Powys's formulation of the typical plot of philosophic romance is Pater's *Marius the Epicurean*, which was published in 1885 and subtitled 'A Philosophic Romance'. Powys's first attempt at a novel was an 'interminable and totally unpublishable story'.[1] He knew the sort of thing he wanted to say, but not how to say it. He needed a framework of ideas, a thematic structure, to give his novels shape. He found his thematic structure in *Marius the Epicurean*, and it enabled him to write *Wood and Stone*.

According to a passage in *Autobiography*, Powys had no knowledge of the works of Walter Pater before he graduated from Cambridge in 1894, the year of Pater's death. When the extensive influence of Pater on the Aesthetic Movement of the 1880s and 1890s is taken into account, as well as his considerable if controversial status as academic and man of letters at Oxford, Powys's ignorance of him may seem surprising, especially in an aspiring littérateur. Powys himself remarks upon the oddity:

> It is queer to think that it was not until I left Cambridge – and this alone indicates the kind of cultural lacunæ which existed in our circle – that I so much as even heard of Walter Pater.[2]

It may be that Powys is doing his circle an injustice; the initial shock of *Studies in the History of the Renaissance*, and particularly its notorious 'Conclusion', had long passed – the work had been published before Powys was out of his cradle. Also, Pater's popularity seems to have become widespread only after his death: during the second half of the 1890s and the whole of the 1900s Pater's principal works were to be constantly reissued, until they were collected in the Library Edition of 1910. Moreover, in *Autobiography* Powys portrays himself as having been sheltered from contemporary literature both at home and at his public school: his reading of nineteenth century literature seems to have been restricted to the staple Victorian bourgeois diet that included for its main course Walter Scott, Wordsworth, and Tennyson. At Corpus Christi he read History for his degree and augmented his English literary studies only by reading Browning, whom he learnt to detest, and Matthew Arnold.[3] At the end of the account of his undergraduate time at Cambridge, Powys declares:

> I did not read a single volume of the least importance to me all the while I was there.[4]

During the next few years, however, Powys encountered the work of contemporary writers, including that of Thomas Hardy, Oscar Wilde, and Yeats.[5] He was discovering with evident enthusiasm a literature that offered a vastly different view of art, society, religion, and morality, from that acceptable to the conventional, provincial Victorian middle class, about whose tastes and values Powys was frequently to complain. Among the writers whose work Powys first read at that time was Walter Pater. By 1902 Powys speaks of him as 'the most valuable of our modern prose writers'.[6]

Powys mentions his admiration for Pater in several places in his non-fictional writings. In *Autobiography* he talks of Pater as one of the 'great imaginative spirits', and later describes himself in America during the years of the First World War as 'a lecturing idealist who admired Walter Pater'.[7] In *The Meaning of Culture* (1929) Powys says of Pater: 'No writer conveys more subtle mastery... of the habit of imaginative concentration'. He recognises that Pater has become unfashionable, that his 'methods of style and treatment' may seem 'antiquated and even affected', but insists that 'the stimulus afforded by [his] noble and meticulous fastidiousness is second to none'.[8] In 1939 Powys complains that 'Pater is wickedly neglected nowadays', and continues: 'He is still my Master. He is still to me... the beautifullest of all our writers'.[9]

Powys's debt to Walter Pater is apparent in many places and ways. Almost in any volume of Pater one will come across sentiments, characters, quotations, and ideas that Powys makes use of. Most of the classical allusions in Powys's novels, for instance, come not directly from the classical authors (I doubt if Powys ever read most of them), but were recalled, often inaccurately, from the writings of Pater.[10] As late as 1942 Powys confessed that he was still taking many tags from Pater.[11]

Powys's debt to Pater, however, has received surprisingly little critical attention. In an essay entitled "Style and the Man" Bernard Jones seeks to show that Powys's prose style owes much to that of Pater,[12] but while he establishes Powys's admiration for Pater by quoting several passages from Powys's critical and autobiographical writings from 1915 to 1934, most of the passages that he quotes suggest that Powys's admiration is primarily for other factors than that of prose style. Indeed, Jones never seriously attempts to compare the prose styles of Pater and Powys. He constantly asserts the stylistic debt without providing any evidence of it. Such an oversight is less surprising, however, when it is recognised that Powys's debt to Pater is not stylistic but intellectual. Bernard Jones is drawn towards that perception in places, in spite of the ostensible subject of his essay, but, perhaps because it lies outside his brief, he does not seek to establish the nature, extent, and significance of the intellectual debt.

I do not wish to present a detailed comparison of the prose styles of Pater and Powys, but I do suggest that most readers, examining representative samples of their work, will be more struck by differences than similarities. Pater's style suggests an analogy with sculpture: it has the symmetry and grace of classical sculpture, but is essentially static. Max Beerbohm summed it up rather well when he accused Pater of treating English 'as a dead language', performing a 'sedulous ritual wherewith he laid out every sentence as in a shroud – hanging, like a widower, long over its marmoreal beauty, or ever he could lay it at length in his book, its sepulchre'.[13]

Powys's prose, by contrast, is almost never static. It is always hurrying on, often with a hastiness of expression that derives from the urge to proceed enthusiastically with the narrative or argument: the speaking voice of the storyteller and the rhetoric of the impromptu lecturer are everywhere discernible.

But whatever the relationship between their prose styles, there was a great deal else that Powys undoubtedly owed to Pater. Fundamental to Pater's creed (as Graham Hough points out in *The Last Romantics*) is the Heraclitean flux. Hough argues that what Pater really wants to attack 'is the notion of an absolute and unchanging truth; and for this he wants to substitute a theory of development and emergence'.[14] Powys had seized upon the same starting-point in the lectures on Pater that he gave in 1903 as part of a course offered by the Cambridge University Extension Delegacy on representative prose writers of the nineteenth century. The syllabus for the course, which was written, as was customary, by the lecturer himself, was issued in 1902, and in that syllabus Powys calls Pater the most valuable of modern prose writers 'because his writings contain a philosophy of life, which... is the expression, through the writings of one man, of feelings and tendencies present in vague outline in the sensibilities of the most refined children of the age'.[15] Pater builds up, says Powys, 'a new system of independent philosophy', and the fundamental concept in that philosophy is 'Relativity':

> He starts by pointing to the Relativity of all things, to the changeableness of all things, to the doctrine of Heraclitus... But upon this metaphysical scepticism, reducing all mental impressions to a sequence of dissolving

fabrics, Pater superimposes a stately edifice of his own. This is a modern Hedonism, a new Epicureanism – 'Follow,' it says, 'each experience that offers itself – each experience will bring its approximate, its relative, Truth, the only Truth man can know.'

'Truth,' he says later, 'is relative to the individual.'

The substance of the first lecture is concerned with Pater's concept of relativity and its implications for religious practice and belief. In the second lecture Powys develops a description of Pater's 'philosophy of experience', and argues that 'the use of the senses as vehicles of Truth is what he teaches, the only Truth we can reach in this life':

> Truth... is not only relative to the general consciousness of the race, that is to say to the mind of Man, it is further relative to the consciousness of the individual, that is to say to the mind of the particular man. This relativity makes him fastidious and exacting with regard to outside objects, so that there shall be no conventional estimate, no formal barrier, between himself and the world without him, so that he should concern himself only with what has a vivid and distinct existence for him.

He goes on to describe the value to the individual of a subjective interpretation of works of art: Pater's new mode of criticism is 'creative' and provides 'important practical evidence of his philosophy'. Pater's style is to be valued not so much for its exquisite quality, pleasing though that may be, as for its embodying 'the temperament as well as the opinions which it has to express'; his style has 'a concealed power which saves and protects it from the charge of preciosity' (a remark that might be taken to imply some uneasiness about Pater's style).

He then returns to Pater's 'central idea':

> we are to value the experience of each moment for its own sake, and with trained faculties of acquisition and discrimination to gather a richer, and ever richer harvest of memories, so that at the end of life – when face to face with the unknown – we may cry our 'Vixi!' thankfully.

Those aspects of Pater that Powys chooses to deal with in the lectures indicate clearly the nature of Powys's interest in Pater, and the importance of Pater in providing the keystones for the elaborate philosophy of sensationalism that Powys was later to develop. The relativity of truth, the sceptical attitude towards religious belief, the subjective interpretation of life and art, the emphasis on key moments of experience and on the accumulated memories of them, permeate all of Powys's subsequent writings, philosophical, critical, and fictional.

Powys's first published novel, *Wood and Stone*, appeared in 1915. Its main theme is the conflict of two apparently irreconcilable sets of principles that are embodied in what Powys labels 'the mythology of power' and 'the mythology of sacrifice'. The main source of the idea, and of its articulation in Powys's novel, is Pater's *Marius the Epicurean*, a work that Powys, according to *Autobiography*, first read in the mid-1890s during his residence in Southwick. He did not immediately appreciate Pater's philosophical romance: 'the devil a word of it could I grasp,' he comments, and again complains about the poverty of his education at Cambridge.[16] By the time of writing *Wood and Stone* Powys had clearly come to grasp a great deal of it, for it everywhere informs the thematic structure of Powys's novel.

Marius the Epicurean traces the philosophical education of a young man called Marius in Italy in the second century AD. It depicts Marius's progress from a simple and traditional pagan background, where religion is of importance primarily in its domestic aspects; through his first school, where he comes under the influence of Heraclitean philosophy; to his stay in Rome, where he is impressed, though not satisfied, by the Epicurean stoicism of Marcus Aurelius; and finally to an encounter with primitive Christianity, whose moral goodness he recognises, although he retains a sceptical view towards Christian dogma.

The turning-point in Marius's dissatisfaction with Aurelian stoicism comes when he witnesses a sadistic spectacle in the Roman arena, in which animals are tortured and sacrificed for the delectation of the public. Pater uses the episode as an opportunity to comment on a comparable injustice and lack of compassion in Victorian society:

> The long chapter of the cruelty of the Roman public shows may, perhaps, leave with the children of the modern world a feeling of self-complacency. Yet it might seem well to ask ourselves – it is always well to do so, when we read of the slave-trade, for instance, or of great religious persecutions on this side or on that, or of anything else which raises in us the question, 'Is thy servant a dog, that he should do this thing?' – not merely, what germs of feeling we may entertain which, under fitting circumstances, would induce us to the like; but, even more practically, what thoughts, what sorts of considerations, may be actually present to our minds such as might have furnished us, living in another age, and in the midst of those legal crimes,

with plausible excuses for them: each age in turn, perhaps, having its own peculiar point of blindness, with its consequent peculiar sin – the touchstone of an unfailing conscience in the select few.[17]

In *Wood and Stone* Powys expresses the connection that Pater suggests between ancient sadism and modern social injustice by associating the 'legal crime' of tyrannical capitalism with the sadism of the 'Promoter of Companies' Mortimer Romer and his daughter Gladys. Powys's adoption of Pater's analogy is apparent in several ways. There is the name 'Romer'. There is Mortimer's joy in manipulating people as a demonstration of his absolute power over them:

He indeed pursued his main purpose, which was the acquiring of power, with an unscrupulousness worthy of a Roman emperor.[18]

There is the consistently sadistic treatment by both Mortimer and Gladys of the dependent orphan girl Lacrima (whose name is of course Latin for 'tear'). Among several passages where the Roman analogy is sustained, there is the scene at Caesar's Quarry, where Lacrima is taken by Gladys so that she can be left at the mercy of a brutish farmer to whom she is forced by Mortimer to become engaged. The farmer's name is Goring, and the quarry is described as a 'cavernous arena' (565). The implicit analogue is clearly the raping of helpless virgins by bulls in ancient Roman arenas as an enacting of the Europa myth. The encounter is watched by Gladys 'with as much ease as if she had been a Drusilla or a Livia, seated in the Roman amphitheatre' (566).

In *Marius the Epicurean*, after his repulsion at the cruelty of Roman public spectacle, Marius comes to recognise, through his experience of the Christian community, the need to feel compassion for suffering humanity. Charity must be added to an acceptance of man's helpless condition. Even in a perfect society there would still be death and suffering, but 'what we need in the world, over against that, is a certain permanent and general power of compassion – humanity's standing force of self-pity – as an elementary ingredient of our social atmosphere, if we are to live in it at all'.[19] In Chapter 8 of *Wood and Stone*, which is entitled 'The Mythology of Sacrifice', Vennie Seldom, who is a young woman of strong religious leaning, makes an impassioned plea for the necessity of Christianity:

'Do you think'... 'that if we were able to hear the weeping of all those who suffer and have suffered since the beginning of the world, we could endure the idea of going on living? It would be too much! The burden of those tears would darken the sun and hide the moon. It is only His presence in the midst of us, – His presence, coming in from outside, that makes it possible for us to endure and have patience.' (153)

Without belief in Christianity, she suggests, there can be only despair, madness, and suicide for those who feel compassion for suffering humanity. The acutely sensitive stonemason James Andersen, who is in love with Lacrima, is like Vennie a strongly compassionate person, but unlike Vennie cannot assent to Christianity. Both Vennie and James escape the oppression of the mythology of power only by becoming sacrificial victims. After an episode in which she feels an overwhelming revulsion against the physical world, Vennie retires to a convent, while James's despair leads him into madness and death. The problem that the novel thus poses as part of its central theme is that of withstanding the mythology of power in its extreme and morally intolerable form (as represented by the Romers) without yielding entirely to the mythology of sacrifice (as represented in Vennie's voluntary seclusion from the world or James's self-annihilation).

The Paterian scheme provides a link between two important strands of the novel, a link that Glen Cavaliero, in *John Cowper Powys: Novelist*, seems to over-look:

> the two main themes of the novel, the tyranny of the Romers, father and daughter, over their financial dependants, and the mental breakdown and collapse of the stonemason James Andersen, bear little relation to each other.[20]

In terms of the dramatic integration of the two strands in a realist fiction, Cavaliero's reservation is perhaps not unjustified, but in terms of the characters' functional relationships in a philosophic romance, the criticism is unfounded. The thematic problem set by *Wood and Stone* is precisely that faced by Marius, who values compassion and sees it exemplified in the Christian community, but whose philosophical sophistication and scepticism cannot allow him to assent wholeheartedly to Christian theological doctrine. Marius's final thoughts clearly represent Pater's own solution to the dilemma:

> Surely, the aim of a true philosophy must lie, not in futile efforts towards

the complete accommodation of man to the circumstances in which he chances to find himself, but in the maintenance of a kind of candid discontent, in the face of the very highest achievement; the unclouded and receptive soul quitting the world finally, with the same fresh wonder with which it had entered the world still unimpaired, and going on its blind way at last with the consciousness of some profound enigma in things, as but a pledge of something further to come.[21]

In *Wood and Stone* there are two representatives of Pater's position. The first is Taxater, partly modelled on the philosopher and theologian John William Williams, whom Powys refers to in *Autobiography* as 'The Catholic'.[22] But if the personality of Taxater owes much to 'The Catholic' his philosophic position suggests an affinity with Pater. He remains outside the main action of the novel, providing, as his name suggests, a detached assessment of people and events. He is 'a gentleman of independent means', and writes for philosophical journals:

Mr. Taxater's written works were, however, but a trifling portion of his personality. His intellectual interests were as rich and varied as those of some great humanist of the Italian Renaissance, and his personal habits were as involved and original as his thoughts were complicated and deep.

He was perpetually engaged in converting the philosopher in him to Catholicism, and the Catholic in him to philosophy – yet he never permitted either of these obsessions to interfere with his enjoyment of life. (18-19)

Because Taxater can easily avoid personal and economic relations with the Romers, he is never forced to compromise his independence of them, which in terms of the novel's action implies an evasion of practical engagement with the novel's thematic problem. The subtle ambiguity of his position is comfortably maintained to the end.

The other representative of Pater's position, and the true hero of the novel, is Maurice Quincunx. A quincunx, which is a pattern of points like that of the dots in the figure 5 on dice, is usually applied to architectural or horticultural configurations, but for Powys the word is associated with the structure of the personality. In *The Art of Happiness,* for instance, he writes of the required 'moral unction in a man', in regard to his treatment of a woman, as 'an ambiguous quincunx, compounded of one part pity, one part reason, and three parts pride'.[23] The quincunx in its correct form – with the right measure of qualities in the right relationship – therefore suggests a balanced personality. Maurice Quincunx's Christian name is of course simply a modern form of 'Marius'.

At the outset of the novel, Quincunx rejects absolutely both the mythology of power and the mythology of sacrifice: Mr Romer and the Church are 'the two subjects' about which Quincunx holds 'dangerously strong views' (17). Over the course of the novel, as he becomes more and more set upon by the Romers, both because he is financially dependent on them and because he loves Lacrima, his philosophic education undergoes a development parallel to that of Marius. Though his character owes little superficially to Marius, he is taught by experience to qualify and modify his philosophy along lines significantly similar to those followed by Pater's hero.

Although Quincunx hates Mortimer Romer and all that he stands for, his philosophic scepticism, and especially his dislike of doctrine, prevent his having any sympathy for the socialist movement that is gaining support among Romer's employees. Instead, after he has been forced by Romer into an occupation that he detests, he adopts a stoical position. He is even prepared to see Lacrima married to Goring rather than to alter the equilibrium of his philosophical detachment from worldly cares:

> 'Of course we know how outrageous it is that such a marriage should be forced on you. But, after all, you and I are above these absurd popular superstitions about all these things... After all, what is this business of being married to people and bearing them children? It doesn't affect your soul. As old Marcus Aurelius says, our bodies are nothing! They are wretched corpses, anyway, dragged hither and thither by our imprisoned souls... You will always have, as that honest fellow Epictetus says, your own soul to retire into, whatever happens...' (305-6)

The sentiments are precisely those that Marius finds in Aurelius's *Meditations*: 'the true interest of the spirit must ever be to treat the body – well! as a corpse attached thereto, rather than as a living companion'; and 'the privilege is yours of retiring into yourself whensoever you please'.[24]

Lacrima's shocked reaction to those words makes Quincunx regret his callousness. In a flash of illumination he recognises the need for compassion. In itself, however, a transient feeling of unselfish pity is insufficient to alter radically Quincunx's refusal to take any positive action to change his own or Lacrima's circumstances. The need to put his new-found compassion to some practical purpose is not brought home to him until near the end of the novel. In Chapter 25, which is entitled 'Metamorphosis', Powys suddenly introduces new and apparently irrelevant characters to the novel. The whole episode of the circus's arrival and Old Flick's attempt, in a secluded grassy hollow, to train the orphan Dolores as a dancing-girl is, to say the least, highly contrived and most improbable even for the improbable world of *Wood and Stone*; but the purpose of the contrivance is clear enough: it is to bring about the conversion of Quincunx from the essentially callous and self-centred creed of classical stoicism to a compassionate and outgoing New Epicureanism. He has to complete the pattern of philosophical education that is undergone by Marius and advocated by Pater in the text from which Powys takes the organising ideas of his novel.[25]

Quincunx's 'drift towards appalling moral disaster' (650) in condoning the marriage of Lacrima and Goring is arrested by the sight of Dolores, who is being led along the road past Quincunx's cottage by Old Flick:

The child's beauty struck him with a shock that almost took his breath away. There was something about the haunting expression of her gaze as she turned it upon him that roused an overpowering flood of tenderness and pity in untouched abysses of his being...

The child's look had indeed the same effect upon Mr. Quincunx that the look of his Master had upon the fear-stricken Apostle, in the hall of Caiaphas the high priest. In one heart-piercing stab it brought to his overpowered consciousness a vision of all the victims of cruelty who had ever cried aloud for help since the generations of men began their tragic journey. (658-60)

Quincunx is thus turned away from moral disaster first by an æsthetic response: as so often in Pater's writings, beauty awakens ethical impulses in its percipient. Second, there is the overwhelming feeling of pity, which is a concomitant, or perhaps a component, of the æsthetic reaction. The experience is represented as analogous to the moment of religious conversion or extreme religious conviction: the girl becomes for Quincunx as powerful a symbol as the suffering Christ, and he re-enters his cottage 'like a man under a blinding illumination':

So must the citizen of Tarsus have looked, when he staggered into the streets of Damascus. (666)

Quincunx then pursues the girl and her keeper. He frightens off Old Flick, and adopts Dolores. Sympathy for children, which Marius takes as a token of the Epicureanism of the very poor, and which he calls a kind of 'secular gold',26 thus becomes the means whereby Quincunx completes his philosophical education:

> The sudden transformation of the timid recluse into a formidable man of action did not end with his triumphant retirement to his familiar domain. Some mysterious fibre in his complicated temperament had been struck, and continued to be struck, by the little Dolores, which not only rendered him indifferent to personal danger, but willing and happy to encounter it. (666)

Shortly afterwards Quincunx resolves to defy the Romers, and to escape to a new life with Lacrima and Dolores. Quincunx is rejuvenated, and Lacrima regains her joy in life; the mood in which they sail away from Weymouth is one of exultation. They quit the world of the Romers in a frame of mind that accords with the closing remarks of *Marius the Epicurean* about the aim of a true philosophy. Lacrima feels like one 'liberated from the tomb'; her emancipation is 'like suddenly becoming a child again – a child with power to enjoy the very things that children so often miss' (704). Everything that she sees around her pleases her. The uncertainty of the future does not bother her, for she has 'the true Pariah tendency to lie back with arms outstretched upon the great tide, and let it carry her whither it pleased', but she thinks it probable that they will find happiness (705). In other words, she is like Pater's 'unclouded and receptive soul':

> quitting the world finally, with the same fresh wonder with which it had entered the world still unimpaired, and going on its blind way at last with the consciousness of some profound enigma in things, as but a pledge of something further to come.27

Quincunx largely shares her mood, but retains certain doubts about how easily they will get on when they are married. He is aware that cruelty and vulgarity will still surround them, but he is filled with resolution to make a cheerful best of things. In Pater's words, he realises where 'the aim of a true philosophy' must lie:

not in futile efforts towards the complete accommodation of man to the circumstances in which he chances to find himself, but in the maintenance of a kind of candid discontent, in the face of the very highest achievement.[28]

The Paterian thematic structure of *Wood and Stone* recurs in various ways throughout Powys's novels. So rich and adaptable is the pattern, that in most of the rest of his novels Powys is enabled to focus on different and sometimes alternative – but still closely related – aspects of it. Although the cult of sensationalism, whose form Powys also owes in large part to Pater, comes increasingly to reinforce New Epicureanism as the life-sustaining philosophy-religion in the succeeding novels, *Wood and Stone* remains the structural and intellectual starting-point for the other novels, as *Marius the Epicurean* remains Powys's theoretical basis for the philosophic romance: if the flesh in Powys's novels is the product of his own fecund imagination, the skeleton remains an inheritance from Pater. The typical story in Powys's novels is that of a sensitive individual learning the right philosophical standpoint both through introspection and through painful experience in a predominantly hostile social world: life is a quest, and its Holy Grail is true philosophy, the aim of which is to allow the individual at the end of his life to shout out his 'Vixi', or at least to enable him to live in the hope that he will do so.

Powys was much more ambitious than Pater. He felt the urge to dramatise the intellectual pattern, to develop the philosophic romance into a form of the novel. Pater's *Marius the Epicurean* is curiously lacking in drama, for all the dramatic possibilities of the scenes and conflicts that he presents. Pater's work reads more like a treatise than a novel. Pater is essentially an essayist, whereas Powys is a true novelist, as he reveals, with more success than has been generally acknowledged, in his first published novel.

After *Wood and Stone* Powys made several other attempts, with varying success, to dramatise the Paterian plot. The next three attempts are largely failures. In *Rodmoor* Powys does not sustain a consistent and convincing narrative voice. He writes in the manner of other writers: of Henry James at the beginning; elsewhere in the manner of Conrad; and elsewhere again in the manner of melodramatic Gothic romance. The explanation of the failure may lie in his very search for a new method of dramatising the pattern of ideas he wanted to express. *After My Fashion* and *Ducdame* are further failures, and in any case are essentially slight.

With *Wolf Solent* Powys finally succeeds admirably in his attempt to dramatise the philosophic education of a central figure, to dramatise the Paterian scheme of the isolated hero trying to come to terms with the conflicting, fleeting, and above all unreliable impressions that he has of the world around him. At the end of the novel, the image of the buttercup field is a version of the 'secular gold' that Pater mentions at the end of *Marius the Epicurean*: that is to say, a New Epicurean attitude of mind. To reach that state, Wolf has to undergo many painful and disconcerting experiences.

The most ambitious and most remarkable expression of the Paterian plot is *A Glastonbury Romance*, where the complex dramatic action and the theoretical elements of the philosophic romance are beautifully synthesised in the perfect metaphor of the Grail quest.

Weymouth Sands, æsthetically perhaps the most pleasing of Powys's novels, can be viewed as a set of lyrical variations on the Paterian theme. With *Maiden Castle*, which some critics have seen as a falling-off of power after the previous three major novels, Powys completed the series of philosophical romances to which he gave contemporary settings. In his later fiction, while retaining many fragments of the Paterian plot, he developed new thematic structures. But with the abandoning of philosophic romance as he had developed it up to *Maiden Castle*, Powys also abandoned coherence.

In a letter to Louis Wilkinson, dated 5 October 1944, Powys makes a revealing comment on his method of plotting:

> I... painfully, laboriously, lengthily build up (I speak both of my tracts *and* my long romances) a sort of foundation, and on top that a sort of scaffolding, *both very simple* – including all the Main Characters & where they live, or all the main theses, propositions & contentions & where they end! *Then* I let *the chance moment* have its way – have its way with the characters, have its way with the ideas![29]

There is no mention of 'story', it should be noted, or plot in the usual sense. His conception at the outset involves (a) characters; (b) place; and (c) theses, propositions, and contentions, and where they end. The plots of Powys's best novels – or romances, as he is still calling them in 1944 – are essentially Paterian plots, the plots of philosophic romance. After dispensing with the type of scaffolding that was so serviceable in the building of *Wolf Solent, A Glastonbury Romance, Weymouth Sands*, and *Maiden Castle*, Powys's fiction becomes diffuse: the sprawling sites may still be interesting to wander among, but they do not constitute the stately edifices of his best philosophic romances.

NOTES

1. *Autobiography*, The Bodley Head, 1934, p. 314.
2. *Autobiography*, p. 181.
3. *Autobiography*, p. 181.
4. *Autobiography*, p. 201.
5. *Autobiography*, pp. 220-1, 224-5.
6. 'Syllabus of a course of twelve lectures on representative prose writers of the nineteenth century', Cambridge, 1902, Lecture 10. Hereafter referred to as *Camb.Syll.1902(iii)*.
7. *Autobiography*, pp. 285, 567.
8. *The Meaning of Culture*, New York: Norton, 1929, p. 30.
9. *Letters to Nicholas Ross*, Rota, 1971, p. 9 (9 November 1939).
10. For a list of allusions in *Wood and Stone, Rodmoor, Ducdame,* and *Wolf Solent*, see the Appendix to my 'The Allusiveness of John Cowper Powys in his First Four Novels', MA dissertation, University of Wales, 1980.
11. *Letters of John Cowper Powys to Louis Wilkinson 1935-1956*, Macdonald, 1958, p. 109 (13 May 1942). Hereafter referred to as *JCP-LW*.
12. Bernard Jones, 'Style and the Man', in Belinda Humfrey (ed.), *Essays on John Cowper Powys*, Cardiff, 1972, pp. 149-177.
13. Quoted in J.H. Buckley, *The Victorian Temper*, 1952, p. 178.
14. Graham Hough, *The Last Romantics*, 1949, p. 141.
15. *Camb.Syll.1902(iii)*, Lecture 10. The quotations that follow are taken from Lectures 10 and 11.
16. *Autobiography*, p. 232.
17. Walter Pater, *Marius the Epicurean*, Library Edition, 1910, Vol. 1, p. 242.
18. *Wood and Stone*, New York: Arnold Shaw, 1915, p. 10. All further references are to this edition, and the page numbers are given in parentheses after quotations in the text. (The London: Village Press edition, 1974, is identical in pagination.)
19. *Marius the Epicurean*, Vol. 2, p. 182.
20. Glen Cavaliero, *John Cowper Powys: Novelist,* Oxford, 1973, p. 22.
21. *Marius the Epicurean*, Vol. 2, p. 220.
22. See *Autobiography*, pp. 280ff.
23. *The Art of Happiness*, The Bodley Head, 1935. Maurice Quincunx at first lacks the element of pity, and is accordingly too proud, i.e., too selfish. Powys undoubtedly took the word 'quincunx' from Sir Thomas Browne's *The Garden of Cyrus*. Powys's use of the quincunx as a model of personality bears an interesting resemblance to Jung's model of the psyche; see, for instance, Jolande Jacobi, *The Psychology of C.G. Jung*, 7th ed., 1968, esp. pp. 10-30.
24. *Marius the Epicurean*, Vol.2, pp. 53, 37-8.
25. Glen Cavaliero is certainly mistaken in his assessment of Quincunx, who he claims is 'described with such discerning humour for much of the novel's length' but is 'revealed as chillingly selfish in the final count' (op.cit., p. 26). The description seems much more appropriate to Luke Andersen.
26. *Marius the Epicurean*, Vol. 2, p. 181.
27. *Marius the Epicurean*, Vol. 2, p. 220.
28. *Marius the Epicurean*, Vol. 2, p. 220.

29. *JCP-LW*, p. 160.

This essay is a revised version of an article that was first published in *The Powys Review,* no. 18, 1986, pp. 29-38.

JOE BOULTER

The Inmates, Deleuze/ Guattari, Foucault, and Madness

This essay will argue that there are close analogies between Powys's ideas and those of Foucault and Deleuze/ Guattari. Both Powys and the most consistent forms of postmodern theory take a pragmatist position: Powys was influenced by William James,[1] and the link between pragmatism and deconstruction has been described by Richard Rorty.[2] (In a less obvious link, Powys influenced Henry Miller, who influenced Deleuze/ Guattari).[3] In pragmatism subject/object dualism, where symbol systems describe the world with varying degrees of success, is replaced by the idea of symbol systems constructing worlds, which cannot be validated through correspondence to anything else.[4] The idea of measuring the individual's world vision against the world itself is replaced by the idea of many world versions and no world.[5]

In this essay I use this pragmatist model to explore the analogies between Powys's treatment of madness and Deleuze/ Guattari's and Foucault's. Madness is an effective site for the debate between pragmatism and dualism, as seen when Deleuze/ Guattari say that 'Freud doesn't like schizophrenics' because 'They mistake words for things' (*AO*, 23). Here Freud's position is characterised as dualist, and the schizophrenics' as pragmatist. I would also contend that the pragmatist model is the best starting point for interpreting

Powys's works as a whole.

In Will Self's "The Quantity Theory of Insanity", the quantity theory states that 'there is only a fixed proportion of sanity available in any given society at any given time'.[6] The implication is that madness is a necessary part of the discursive construction of social norms. It doesn't matter who is designated as mad or in what way, but the rest can fix their normality by othering the mad.

This is the attitude to madness found in Foucault, who is committed to a strong nominalism in the human sciences in which 'the types of objects in their domains were not already demarcated, but came into existence only contemporaneous with the discursive formations that made it possible to talk about them.'[7] Foucault is insistent about this in his account of sexuality.[8] Similarly, he sees madness as a variable social construction rather than an absolute truth, and sees the construction of madness as part of the construction of rationality. He refers in his 'Preface' to *'that other form of madness, by which men, in an act of sovereign reason, confine their neighbours, and communicate and recognize each other through the merciless language of non-madness'*.[9] The confinement of the mad and the mutual recognition and communication of the sane are seen to be part of the same process. Foucault says that 'power and knowledge directly imply one another'.[10] In terms of his discussion of sexuality this means that he is concerned to 'account for the fact that it is spoken about, to discover who does the speaking, the positions and viewpoints from which they speak, the institutions which prompt people to speak about it and which store and distribute the things that are said', 'to locate the forms of power, the channels it takes, and the discourses it permeates'.[11] Powys's 'Prefatory Note' to *The Inmates* indicates that the concerns of the novel are going to be precisely with power's use of madness. The designation of some world versions as mad becomes a political tactic in the preservation of the existing institutions of power and in the individual's own entry into these institutions. Powys tells us that 'certain dominant attitudes to life, to nature and to the cosmos, which, though contrary to all the accepted notions of the conventional minds who make up the world's judgment, have a deep abiding philosophic truth'. However,

> this 'truth', this Philosophy of the Demented, is naturally under the ban of our authorities in Church and State. And being condemned at the top level

it is very noticeable that it is anathema to the underlings, whose personal power and glory depend, of course, as they mount up, on the conventional ideas they have at last, after many rungs of the careerist-ladder, come to embody and represent. (*I*, vii)

In *The Inmates* itself, Powys repeatedly makes direct connections between the designation of madness and the preservation of institutions of political power. Mrs Squeeze mentions the likely fact that Dr Echetus will become a Lord, and we are told that at Glint Hall 'experiments on living dogs were carried on that Betsy Squeeze regarded as a scientist's shortest cut to the peerage' (*I*, 16, 18). Tenna Sheer's father, who is responsible for her confinement, is also a 'Sir'. The connection between his social power and his power to confine is symbolised in his name, 'Sir Warden' (*I*, 38, 107). Though Powys argues against the truth of the psychoanalytic world version, *The Inmates* does confirm it to the extent that the confiner and the knight is also the father, and rebellion against society for Osbert Lordy and Tenna takes the form of an attack on the father. This arrangement corresponds to Foucault's description of the madman's relationship to the institutions of reason as that of a minor: 'the asylum would keep the insane in the imperative fiction of the family; the madman remains a minor, and for a long time reason will retain for him the aspect of the Father' (*MC*, 254). Freudian psychoanalysis maintains the minority of the patient by situating his problems in infancy, as part of the familial romance.

The exercise of power by social institutions in *The Inmates* takes the form of confining and silencing those with incompatible world versions. The first images of Glint Hall are of imprisonment: the grounds are 'enclosed by a high and imposing wall' (*I*, 14). The othering process is seen to be directly linked to the preservation of institutions of power in the case of Commander Serius-Ocius, who

> had officially been directed to take a prolonged holiday under Doctor Echetus by reason of a peculiar habit he had fallen into of waylaying Members of Parliament of both parties on their way to Westminster and informing them of the absolute necessity of being more philosophical in their attitude to public affairs if the ship of state was to weather the present storm. (*I*, 144)

John 'Hush' in his own surname illustrates the silencing which is an essential part of the treatment of madness. His confinement is also an explicitly political measure: Hush has asked his guardian to have him certified so that the guardian can serve the government (*I*, 51). The fact that Hush has asked for his own exclusion illustrates Foucault's idea that 'power is not exercised simply as an obligation or a prohibition on those who "do not have it"; it invests them, is transmitted by them and through them'.[12]

Powys's description of the asylum is analogous to Foucault's description of the classical means of dealing with madness as exclusion and confinement, the designation of the mad as nonrational and consequently the delineation of the rational society by the othering of the mad. Reason's exclusion of madness in the classical era is illustrated by Foucault with the redefinition of the madness of the cross:

> It was no longer a matter of requiring human reason to abandon its pride and its certainties in order to lose itself in the great unreason of sacrifice. When classical Christianity speaks of the madness of the Cross, it is merely to humiliate false reason and add luster to the eternal light of truth; the madness of God-in-man's-image is simply a wisdom not recognized by the men of unreason who live in this world. (*MC*, 79)

Even if Roy Porter is right to suggest a different reason from Foucault for the exclusion of the mad, his argument that the classical age acted from 'the Lockean view of the mad' as 'people who, through misassociation of ideas, go desperately awry in their reasoning',[13] still sees the exclusion being made as a means of patrolling the borders of rationality. What is at stake still is what Foucault describes as *'reason's subjugation of non-reason, wresting from it its truth as madness, crime, or disease'* (*MC*, xi-xii).

This use of the designation of madness as a means of asserting rationalism continued in the nineteenth-century shift from the internment of the mad to their treatment. Madness continued, and continues, according to Foucault, to be confined within the construction of mental illness (*MC*, xiv). Foucault 'repeatedly asserts his view that the modern conception of mental illness and the corresponding institution of the asylum have been unknowingly constructed out of elements of the Classical experience of madness.'[14] The development of the idea of madness as something which needs to be cured in the nineteenth century continues to represent madness as without its own validity as a world version. In the nineteenth-century space for curing it, 'madness will never again be able to speak the language of unreason, with all that in it transcends the natural phenomena of disease. It will be entirely enclosed in pathology' (*MC*, 196-7). Powys's treatment of the idea of curing at Glint corresponds to Foucault's description.

Foucault says that the asylum 'organized [...the madman's] guilt; it organized it for the madman as a consciousness of himself [...] it organized it for the man of reason as an awareness of the Other'. '[F]rom the acknowledgement of his status as object, from the awareness of his guilt, the madman was to return to his awareness of himself as a free and responsible subject, and consequently to reason.' For Foucault, in curing the mad, the asylum will try to create a subject which identifies itself as other and from there can proceed to being cured, a process which entails renunciation of the subject's particular world version, by seeing it as a world vision which is flawed, and thus proceeding to normalisation.

This process of normalisation requires the normaliser to have authority (*MC*, 252), and 'Authority, perhaps, would be a better word for the head of Glint than any other' (*I*, 126).[15] It also requires the madman to accept the authority which designates him as mad. This is the position in which we encounter John Hush at the beginning of *The Inmates*: he has asked to be 'Certified'. Deleuze/ Guattari follow Wilhelm Reich in identifying this wish for repression as a desire in itself.[16] It is a desire which Powys represents elsewhere, such as in Isaac Weatherwax's opinion that '"Authority"' '"be the pivot of life upon earth"'. '"When I sees true livin' Authority"', he says, '"I knows vegetables grow, and hens lay, and cattle breed, and poor folk be fed and clothed."'[17] The name 'Weatherwax' has further association with normalisation: Rud Weatherwax was Lassie's trainer. In *Gravity's Rainbow,* Dr Pointsman pursues a dog on which he wants to experiment, telling Roger Mexico, '"we need him as close to normative [...] as possible"'. The dog asks them '"You vere ekshpecting maybe *Lessie?*"'[18]

Deleuze/ Guattari's adoption of Reich's idea of the masses as not deluded by but desiring fascism is consistent with their general project which refuses to dismiss the madman's world version as a distorted world vision. Deleuze/ Guattari criticise psychoanalysis's aim of restoring the madman's sense of self, his ability to say the word 'I', and go so far as to say that the schizo 'is ill because of the oedipalization to which he is made to submit', that 'Our society produces schizos the same way it produces Prell shampoo or Ford cars' (which recalls Foucault's nominalist description of madness as a social construct) (*AO*, 23, 123, 245).

Similarly Powys wants to avoid such a normalisation and preserve the individual world version of the madman. This need to preserve the individual's world version 'in spite of' the social drive to normalise it is the main theme of *In Spite Of: A Philosophy For Everyman* which was published a year later than *The Inmates*, in 1953. Here, Powys declares 'Happy is the man who knows not the difference between orthodoxy and heresy!'[19] The ability not to designate oneself as mad is what is important here. The madman's task is to preserve his own particular madness: 'everyone in the world, even your nearest and dearest, *is a doctor desirous of curing you* – while *your* purpose, absolutely alone as you are in a world far madder than yourself, is to conceal your insanity' (*ISO*, 156).

The strategy which Powys recommends for the madman is to conceal his oddity from everyone else; not to try to reduce it, but simply to cover it up: 'Hide from every living soul that you are, as these normal people call it, "out of your mind", crazy, demented, "funny", "dotty" – there is no lack of words to describe the hostility of the normal towards the abnormal'.[20]

Foucault details in his later work the effects of an increase in communication. 'These practices of surveillance, elicitation, and documentation constrain behaviour precisely by making it more thoroughly knowable or known. But these new forms of knowledge also presuppose new kinds of constraint, which make people's actions visible and constrain them to speak.'[221] Consequently we see a second significance for Hush's surname as hinting at the need to disengage from the institutional practice of power through silence: through his 'Hush' he is resisting the attempt to classify him. At one stage this preservation of power through silence is seen in action: John works out Tamia Cuddle's real name: '"Her name," he thought, "is Mesopotamia"; and instantaneously he decided that he would conceal from Cogent Cuddle that he knew his wife's name' (*I*, 24).

Confession is a central tool of psychoanalysis, and Powys specifically advises against the psychoanalytic confession for the madman, wishing to

> dissuade him from blurting out his secrets to any psychiatrist, or blabbing of them to any doctor, or revealing them in any of those warm, cosy, relaxed,

melting, cushiony confessionals, where our obscure memories of childish knocks and shocks and thrills and chills are dropped like wriggling worms on fish-hooks into a purely imaginary subterranean tank under the floor of our soul, absurdly and paradoxically called, though our jailers know every inch of its mud and its monsters, 'the unconscious' (*ISO*, 128).

What Powys is calling attention to here is the fact that the analyst translates the experience of the madman into the discourse of the unconscious in a normalising process where the othered experience of madness is normalised via the approved mythology of the unconscious. Powys's suspicion of the process is indicated by the fact that in his description the unconscious is presented by psychoanalysis as both question and answer, as the thing which lies beyond the madman's knowledge, and yet simultaneously as the thing which will explain his behaviour because it has been authorised as part of 'reality'. As Powys points out, this puts the analyst in a privileged position of telling the madman what he really feels and dismissing what the madman thinks he feels as an invalid world vision. Madness has become 'An enigma without any truth except that which could reduce it' (*MC*, 198) . In reinterpreting the world version of the madman as a flawed world vision, psychoanalysis takes its place as part of a general post-Renaissance reduction of madness from an ontological to an epistemological level. The threat of another order of being is reduced to a misinterpretation: 'Magic, for example, once violently suppressed as an objectively powerful challenge to religion through its evocation of evil powers, now is regarded as merely a personal delusion that threatens the secular social order.'[22]

Powys, from his pragmatist viewpoint, cannot discard the world version of the madman. He says of Dr Echetus 'that to follow the actual feelings of his patients' afflicted nerves *as they felt them themselves* should be one of the first steps to any real cure was the last thing the famous doctor could imagine or conceive' (*I*, 61). However, what Powys himself proposes for *The Inmates* is a refusal to translate, and a corresponding attention to the madman's own world version, 'a savage avoidance of all the modern psychoanalytical catchwords, whether quasi-popular or pseudo-scientific, as leading us away from the heart of the matter, which is not the cause of the patient's mania but how it feels to himself or herself to suffer from it' (*I*, vi-vii). The aim of the book is 'to defend the crazy ideas of mad people' 'as against the conventional ideas of sane people' (*I*, vii).

Powys's defence of the mad against the sane, especially as it is represented by psychoanalysis, stems from his conception of psychoanalysis as just another world version, without any particular claim to be true. He says, for example, that 'Jung's followers have carried the theory of the Unconscious [to extravagant lengths], a theory that in a hundred years will probably be relinquished as a complete illusion' (*I*, vii). In this suspicion he is close to Deleuze/ Guattari, who characterise Freudian psychoanalysis as a 'belief' (*AO*, 92), and complain that psychoanalysis is failing to innovate in that 'it continues to ask its questions and develop its interpretations from the depths of the Oedipal triangle as its basic perspective, even though today it is acutely aware that this frame of reference is not at all adequate to explain so-called psychotic phenomena' (*AO*, 14, 53).

Deleuze/ Guattari are also close to Powys in their resistance to psychoanalysis's tendency to translate, approving of D. H. Lawrence's reservations about psychoanalysis 'stifling the whole of sexuality as production of desire so as to recast it along entirely different lines', and criticising psychoanalysis's 'forcing the entire interplay of desiring machines to fit within [...] the restricted code of Oedipus.' Instead, they insist that 'A desiring machine and a partial object do not represent anything' (*AO*, 49, 47). Foucault also concludes his study of madness by representing psychoanalysis as suppressing the voices of unreason, arguing that although psychoanalysis has replaced the asylum with the doctor, the powers of the asylum have been concentrated in the doctor (*MC*, 278).

Against what he sees as the modern tendency to identify madness as an invalid take on the world which needs correction, Foucault pits views of madness as having its own validity. His 'book shows an antihistorical character in Foucault's intermittent efforts to evoke madness as it is experienced by the mad themselves.'[23]

In focusing on the validity of the world version of the madman, Foucault contrasts the excluding, confining classical attitude to madness in which it 'has ceased to be [...] an eschatological figure' (*MC*, 35) with the 'integration of madness into medieval and Renaissance existence'. 'Renaissance madness [...] is either the critical ironic inverse of reason or a tragic and horrifying example of monstrous truths. In either case, madness is an integral but disconcerting aspect of human life, essential but by no means welcomed.'[24] Foucault claims that in the Renaissance, 'Madmen led an easy wandering existence' (*MC*, 8). More importantly, their experience was regarded as not just an epistemological error, but as of a different ontological order: 'It is for the other world that the madman sets sail in his fool's boat; it is from the other world that he comes when he disembarks' (*MC*, 11). As another means of emphasising the validity of the madman's world version, Foucault valorises the mad artist (he sees the life of unreason shown in the work of Hölderlin, Nerval, Nietzsche and Artaud) (*MC*, 278) as a source of transgression and intensity.

Like Foucault, and Deleuze/ Guattari who say that 'Madness need not be all breakdown. It may also be breakthrough' (*AO*, 131), Powys stresses the special validity of madness. His attitude corresponds to the pre-classical view as Foucault describes it when he says that we must assume not

> that the abnormal are seeing things falsely while the normal are seeing them as they are, but [...] that Nature has revealed to the abnormal, through various poetical signs and symbolic hallucinations, certain profound secrets of reality which she has concealed from the normal. (*ISO,* 132)

This acceptance of the ideas of the mad as valid world versions is thematised in *The Inmates*, where they are treated as factual as ideas with which we are more familiar. For example, when one inmate claims to be the son of the Flying Dutchman, the narrator accepts his claim, referring to him as 'the son of the great seaman', and 'the son of the Flying Dutchman.' (*I*, 35)

Each of *The Inmates* has their own very different world version, supporting the idea in *In Spite Of* that the mind 'has fearful apprehensions, disgusting memories, appalling visions. And not one single one of these is identical, or even nearly identical, with anyone else's' (*ISO,* 45). This contradicts the classical and modern setting of madness in a binary opposition of reason versus unreason, an opposition which Foucault describes when he shows how a heterogeneous group of people was confined in the classical age. The conflict between pragmatism and dualism is illustrated by the fact that although we see in *The Inmates* that each inmate has a highly individualised world version, they are all confined according to the same opposition of reason and unreason. The confining function of this opposition, its failure to include all possibilities, is symbolised by digitality when John Hush says, '"That's the worst of these electric bulbs" [...] "you can't turn them *down*. You can only turn them *out*"' (*I*,

172). Nelson Goodman draws attention to what here is essentially a distinction between analogue and digital.[25]

The variety of world versions among the inmates is contrasted with the clichedness of Dr Echetus, which is evident in the very phrases which authorise him as 'the famous Doctor Echetus' (*I*, 13). Echetus's combination of authority and banality, which Powys says is reminiscent of a 'competent manager', a 'professional cricketer' or a 'general supervisor' (*I*, 15), can also be contrasted to Foucault's association of artistic originality with madness.

In *The Inmates* the validation of the inmates' world versions is symbolised by their flight from confinement at the end of the novel, and by the death of the man who designated them as mad, Echetus, not at their hands but at the hands of one of his assistants (*I*, 303). In terms of pragmatism, however, in the demonstration of the validity of each world version and of the fact that the designation of madness is based not on some world visions being truer than others by corresponding to reality but on social institutions, the key incident is when the American newcomer mistakes parents of patients for patients themselves (*I*, 295). As in Self's "Ward 9",[26] the fact that those who authorised confinement can be taken for inmates argues against madness existing as an intrinsic quality preceding designation by institutions of power.

In letting his inmates take flight, Powys enacts what Deleuze/ Guattari call 'deterritorialization': the characters of the novel take a 'line of flight'[27] out of the oppositionality by which they have been designated as mad, and by which the institutions which so designated them have constituted themselves as rational. The first image for deterritorialization in Deleuze/ Guattari is the schizo's stroll, and this is presented as alternative to oppositionality, in which 'the self and the non-self, outside and inside, no longer have any meaning whatsoever' (*AO*, 2). Deleuze/ Guattari ask if, rather than translating schizophrenia into Freudian terms, it would not be better to schizophrenize the unconscious (*AO*, 53). The result would be what they describe as 'disjunctive synthesis', 'A disjunction that remains disjunctive, and that still affirms the disjoined terms, that affirms them throughout their entire distance, *without restricting one by the other or excluding the other from the one*' (*AO*, 76). A way of thinking in which different world versions could coexist without striving to exclude each other (as classical and modern attitudes to madness have), would correspond to a nondigital system in which lights would have a position between on and off, gas instead of electric, the position between zero and one represented in *Gravity's Rainbow* by Roger Mexico (as opposed to Ned Pointsman who can only accept either/or).28 In the case of madness, as Foucault shows, and lighting, as Powys indicates, a return to the past gives us metaphors for postmodern theory.

Both Deleuze/ Guattari and Foucault stress the importance of avoiding a repetition of the oppositional structure in resisting institutions of power. The point is not simply to reverse the designation by saying, 'It's not me who's mad, it's you'. It is not the intention of schizoanalysis to resolve the problem of Oedipus, 'Its aim is to de-oedipalize the unconscious' (*AO*, 81).

Foucault also makes a distinction between true resistances to power and those which are 'only a reaction or rebound, forming with respect to the basic domination an underside that is in the end always passive, doomed to perpetual defeat.'29 In order to avoid simply repeating the oppositionality he is attacking, Powys seeks an effect such that

> We declare emphatically and oracularly that we place, as Goethe did, according to Professor Seeley, a thin film of white light under every theory we hold, so that it cannot, even to ourselves, look like anything final, conclusive, or absolute, or appear as the sort of thing for whose 'truth' we would be prepared to quarrel fiercely. 'A *thin film of white light beneath*' every one of our opinions would make clear what our opinions were worth, valuable, certainly, as one play of form and colour among others, *but that is all*. (*ISO*, 92)

In the plot of *The Inmates*, the repeat of oppositionality is avoided. Although Hush speculates about how he would run the asylum (*I*, 47), we do not see the world visions of the mad supersede those of the sane. Instead, the inmates fly the whole rational/ nonrational structure; they quit the oppositional game.

Another aspect of *The Inmates* which prevents it from establishing itself as the true vision of the world in opposition to the institutional rational/ non-rational divide which it deconstructs is its own blatant constructedness. The novel parades its own fictionality, the fact that it itself is simply one of many competing world versions, in many different ways. Just two examples are the choice of names – 'Mr. Frogcastle' is typically unrealistic – and the deliberate reference to a common wish-fulfilment story in an ending in which John and

Tenna run away to join the circus (*I*, 318). By advertising itself as fiction, *The Inmates* guards against establishing itself as the true vision of the world, and consequently remains consistent with the principle that 'Everything depends on the agreement of our minds about reality. That is sanity and everything is relative to that. There is no such thing as what the more simple-minded of our scientists call the "objective world"' (*I*, 245).

In stressing the fact that 'reality is socially constructed', Powys is prefiguring Peter Berger and Thomas Luckmann.[30] According to Berger and Luckmann, social marginality contributes to the de-reification of social reality, reification being man's forgetfulness of his authorship of his own world (ib., 109, 106). '[U]nsuccessful socialization opens up the question of "Who am I?"' (ib., 190). This question in turn leads to '[t]he possibility of "individualism" (that is, of individual choice between discrepant realities and identities)' (ib., 190). The madman epitomises marginality, though with the additional quality that in being confined he reveals more obviously than most outsiders the role of institutions of power in his othering. By showing the othering of the mad as part of the social construction of reality, Powys opens up the possibility of individualism, of the individual making his own selection of constructed roles, rather than accepting the role which socially constructed reality allots to him as mad or normal. This ranging between roles is analogous to the stroll of Deleuze/ Guattari's schizo.

Powys sees support for madness in pragmatism. In *In Spite Of* he refers to 'the staggering mathematical hypothesis of a number of dimensions other than the one with which we are familiar. This indeed is a stroke for the mental liberation of individual man and woman that cannot be overpraised' (*ISO*, 30-31). The scientific possibility of multiple dimensions, referred to in *The Inmates* when Hush thinks of 'an old print his guardian possessed of Bernard De Fontenelle, author of *The Plurality of Worlds*' (*I*, 113), supports the philosophical possibility of a plurality of worlds.

The idea of a plurality of worlds in turn supports a plurality of equally valid world versions (*ISO*, 40, 82-83), and the argument against trying to normalise the mad. Powys says,

> I like to tell myself that one aspect of the Philosophy of the Demented is that daring cosmological theory about a real plurality of worlds; namely the theory of William James that we live in a multiverse rather than a universe.

> Everyone of my inmates is a symbol of some important aspect of its truth which seems to me especially alien to the schoolmaster-taught conventional mind with its passion for unity and oneness. (*I*, viii)

If *The Inmates* represents part of Powys's ongoing argument for pragmatism and against dualism, that argument is also carried on by its characters. *The Inmates*' programme of normalisation involves a conversion to dualism, as seen in Father Toby's assurance that 'the beautiful thing about our cosmic soccer ball is that it is *the all*' (*I*, 240). The inmates, naturally, are on the side of pragmatism, and Commander Serius-Ocius contends that '"it is ridiculous to say that there is only one world. There are as many worlds as there are minds to plunge into matter, and these are beyond counting"' (*I*, 149).

In *The Inmates*, as in Foucault and Deleuze/ Guattari, madness is a site on which the argument between pragmatism and dualism can be conducted. Powys's support for the madman's world version, like that of the postmoderns, stems from an underlying pragmatism. Thus the analogies established between Powys and postmodernism in the case of madness provide a model which might be equally successfully applied to the interpretation of other aspects of Powys's work.

NOTES

1. For example, John Cowper Powys, *The Inmates* (London: Village Press, 1974), viii. Cited hereafter as *I*.
2. Richard Rorty, *Consequences of Pragmatism* (Brighton: Harvester Press, 1982), xviii.
3. Gilles Deleuze/ Félix Guattari, *Anti-Oedipus: Capitalism and Schizophrenia*, trans. Robert Hurley, Mark Seem, Helen R. Lane (London: Athlone Press, 1984), 132. Cited hereafter as *AO*.
4. Rorty, *Consequences of Pragmatism*, xvi.
5. See Nelson Goodman, *Ways of Worldmaking* (Indianapolis: Hackett, 1978), 3, 4.
6. Will Self, "The Quantity Theory of Insanity", *The Quantity Theory of Insanity* (London: Penguin, 1994), 126.
7. Joseph Rouse, "Power/ Knowledge", *The Cambridge Companion to Foucault*, ed. Gary Gutting (Cambridge: Cambridge University Press, 1994), 93.
8. Michel Foucault, *The History of Sexuality*, vol. 1: *An Introduction*, trans. Robert Hurley (London: Penguin, 1984), 48.
9. Michel Foucault, *Madness and Civilization: A History of Insanity in the Age of Reason*, trans. Richard Howard (London: Routledge, 1993), xi. Cited hereafter as *MC*.
10. Michel Foucault, *Discipline and Punish: The Birth of the Prison*, trans. Alan Sheridan (London: Penguin, 1991), 27.
11. Foucault, *The History of Sexuality*, 11.
12. Foucault, *Discipline and Punish*, 27.
13. Gary Gutting, "Foucault and the History of Madness", *The Cambridge Companion to Foucault*, ed. Gary Gutting (Cambridge: Cambridge University Press, 1994), 53.
14. Gutting, "Foucault and the History of Madness", 60.
15. Echetus is typically described as "the head', and 'the master' (*I*, 13, 15).
16. Wilhelm Reich, *The Mass Psychology of Fascism*, trans. Vincent R. Carfagno (London: Souvenir P, 1972), xv. Deleuze/ Guattari, *Anti-Oedipus*, 29, 116, 257.
17. John Cowper Powys, *A Glastonbury Romance* (London: Picador-Pan, 1975), 210.
18. Thomas Pynchon, *Gravity's Rainbow* (London: Picador-Pan, 1975), 44.
19. Powys, *In Spite Of: A Philosophy For Everyman* (London: Macdonald, 1953), 95. Cited hereafter as *ISO*.
20. Powys, *In Spite Of*, 128-9. See Nelson Goodman for the way digitality limits possible options.
21. Rouse, "Power/ Knowledge", 96.
22. Gutting, "Foucault and the History of Madness", 56.
23. Gutting, "Foucault and the History of Madness", 66.
24. Gutting, "Foucault and the History of Madness", 50, 51.
25. Goodman, *Ways of Worldmaking*, 15.
26. Will Self, "Ward 9", *The Quantity Theory of Insanity* (London: Penguin, 1994), 67.
27. Gilles Deleuze/ Félix Guattari, *A Thousand Plateaus: Capitalism and*

Schizophrenia, trans. Brian Massumi (London: Athlone Press, 1988), 9.
  28. Pynchon, *Gravity's Rainbow,* 55.
  29. Foucault, *The History of Sexuality,* 96.
  30. Peter L. Berger and Thomas Luckmann, *The Social Construction of Reality: A Treatise in the Sociology of Knowledge* (London: Penguin, 1971), 13.

This essay appeared in *The Powys Journal,* 7, 1997 (The Powys Society, UK).

J.R.R. Tolkien
The Books, The Films, The Whole Cultural Phenomenon

by Jeremy Mark Robinson

A new critical study of J.R.R. Tolkien, creator of Middle-earth and author of *The Lord of the Rings, The Hobbit* and *The Silmarillion*, among other books.

This new critical study explores Tolkien's major writings (*The Lord of the Rings, The Hobbit, Beowulf: The Monster and the Critics, The Letters, The Silmarillion* and *The History of Middle-earth* volumes); Tolkien and fairy tales; the mythological, political and religious aspects of Tolkien's Middle-earth; the critics' response to Tolkien's fiction over the decades; the Tolkien industry (merchandizing, toys, role-playing games, posters, Tolkien societies, conferences and the like); Tolkien in visual and fantasy art; the cultural aspects of The Lord of the Rings (from the 1950s to the present); Tolkien's fiction's relationship with other fantasy fiction, such as C.S. Lewis and *Harry Potter*; and the TV, radio and film versions of Tolkien's books, including the 2001-03 Hollywood interpretations of *The Lord of the Rings*.

This new book draws on contemporary cultural theory and analysis and offers a sympathetic and illuminating (and sceptical) account of the Tolkien phenomenon. This book is designed to appeal to the general reader (and viewer) of Tolkien: it is written in a clear, jargon-free and easily-accessible style.

754pp ISBN 1-86171-057-7 £25.00 / $37.50

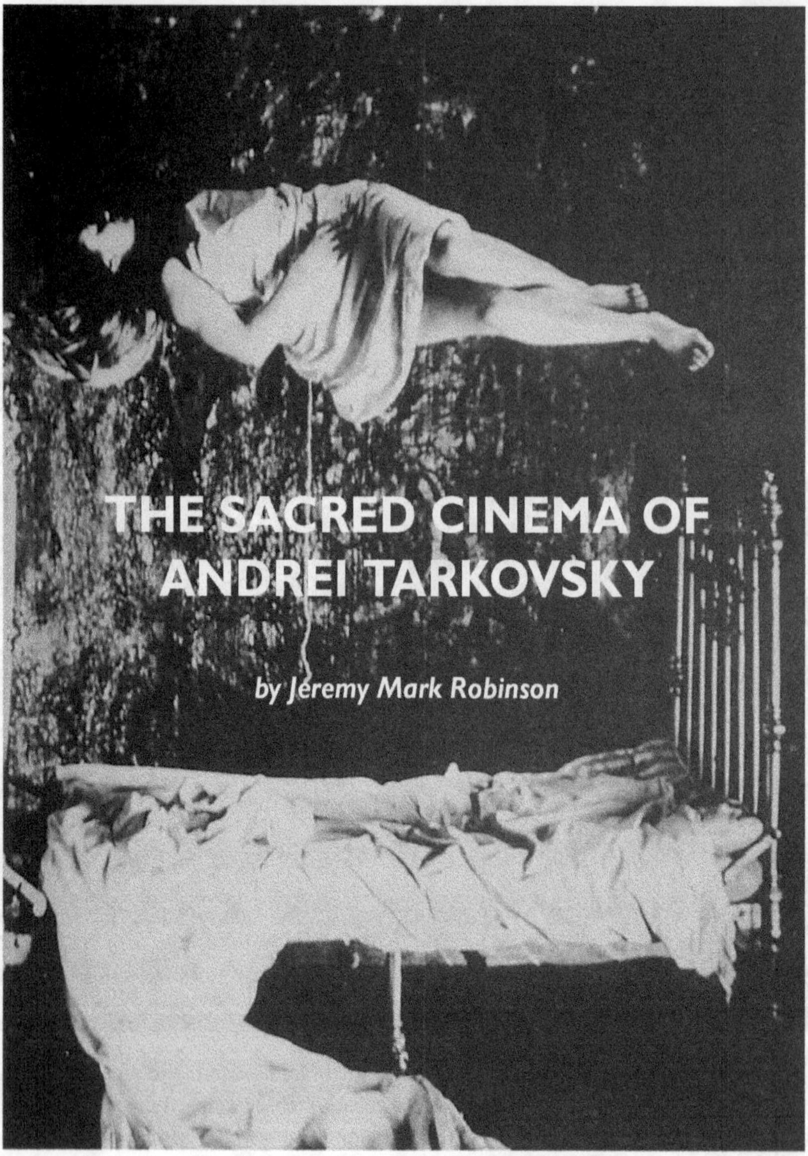

THE SACRED CINEMA OF ANDREI TARKOVSKY

by Jeremy Mark Robinson

A new study of the Russian filmmaker Andrei Tarkovsky (1932-1986), director of seven feature films, including *Andrei Roublyov, Mirror, Solaris, Stalker* and *The Sacrifice*.
This is one of the most comprehensive and detailed studies of Tarkovsky's cinema available. Every film is explored in depth, with scene-by-scene analyses. All aspects of Tarkovsky's output are critiqued, including editing, camera, staging, script, budget, collaborations, production, sound, music, performance and spirituality. Tarkovsky is placed with a European New Wave tradition of filmmaking, alongside directors like Ingmar Bergman, Carl Theodor Dreyer, Pier Paolo Pasolini and Robert Bresson.
An essential addition to film studies.

Illustrations: 150 b/w, 4 colour. 682 pages. First edition. Hardback.

Publisher: Crescent Moon Publishing. Distributor: Gardners Books.

ISBN 1-86171-096-8 (9781861710963) £60.00 / $105.00

The Best of Peter Redgrove's Poetry
The Book of Wonders

by Peter Redgrove, edited and introduced by Jeremy Robinson

Poems of wet shirts and 'wonder-awakening dresses'; honey, wasps and bees; orchards and apples; rivers, seas and tides; storms, rain, weather and clouds; waterworks; labyrinths; amazing perfumes; the Cornish landscape (Penzance, Perranporth, Falmouth, Boscastle, the Lizard and Scilly Isles); the sixth sense and 'extra-sensuous perception'; witchcraft; alchemical vessels and laboratories; yoga; menstruation; mines, minerals and stones; sand dunes; mud-baths; mythology; dreaming; vulvas; and lots of sex magic. This book gathers together poetry (and prose) from every stage of Redgrove's career, and every book. It includes pieces that have only appeared in small presses and magazines, and in uncollected form.

'Peter Redgrove is really an extraordinary poet' (George Szirtes, *Quarto* magazine)
'Peter Redgrove is one of the few significant poets now writing... His 'means' are indeed brilliant and delightful. Technically he is a poet essentially of brilliant and unexpected images...he never disappoints' (Kathleen Raine, *Temenos* magazine).

240pp   ISBN 1-86171-063-1   2nd edition   £19.99 / $29.50

Sex–Magic–Poetry–Cornwall
A Flood of Poems

by Peter Redgrove. Edited with an essay by Jeremy Robinson

A marvellous collection of poems by one of Britain's best but underrated poets, Peter Redgrove. This book brings together some of Redgrove's wildest and most passionate works, creating a 'flood' of poetry. Philip Hobsbaum called Redgrove 'the great poet of our time', while Angela Carter said: 'Redgrove's language can light up a page.' Redgrove ranks alongside Ted Hughes and Sylvia Plath. He is in every way a 'major poet'. Robinson's essay analyzes all of Redgrove's poetic work, including his use of sex magic, natural science, menstruation, psychology, myth, alchemy and feminism.
A new edition, including a new introduction, new preface and new bibliography.

'Robinson's enthusiasm is winning, and his perceptive readings are supported by a very useful bibliography' (*Acumen* magazine)
'*Sex-Magic-Poetry-Cornwall* is a very rich essay... It is like a brightly-lighted box. (Peter Redgrove)
'This is an excellent selection of poetry and an extensive essay on the themes and theories of this unusual poet by Jeremy Robinson' (*Chapman* magazine)

220pp   New, 3rd edition   ISBN 1-86171-070-4   £14.99 / $23.50

THE ART OF ANDY GOLDSWORTHY

COMPLETE WORKS: SPECIAL EDITION
(PAPERBACK and HARDBACK)

by William Malpas

A new, special edition of the study of the contemporary British sculptor, Andy Goldsworthy, including a new introduction, new bibliography and many new illustrations.

This is the most comprehensive, up-to-date, well-researched and in-depth account of Goldsworthy's art available anywhere.

Andy Goldsworthy makes land art. His sculpture is a sensitive, intuitive response to nature, light, time, growth, the seasons and the earth. Goldsworthy's environmental art is becoming ever more popular: 1993's art book *Stone* was a bestseller; the press raved about Goldsworthy taking over a number of London West End art galleries in 1994; during 1995 Goldsworthy designed a set of Royal Mail stamps and had a show at the British Museum. Malpas surveys all of Goldsworthy's art, and analyzes his relation with other land artists such as Robert Smithson, Walter de Maria, Richard Long and David Nash, and his place in the contemporary British art scene.

The Art of Andy Goldsworthy discusses all of Goldsworthy's important and recent exhibitions and books, including the *Sheepfolds* project; the TV documentaries; *Wood* (1996); the New York Holocaust memorial (2003); and Goldsworthy's collaboration on a dance performance.

Illustrations: 70 b/w, 1 colour. 330 pages. New, special, 2nd edition.
Publisher: Crescent Moon Publishing. Distributor: Gardners Books.

ISBN 1-86171-059-3 (9781861710598) (Paperback) £25.00 / $44.00

ISBN 1-86171-080-1 (9781861710802) (Hardback) £60.00 / $105.00

CRESCENT MOON PUBLISHING

ARTS, PAINTING, SCULPTURE

The Art of Andy Goldsworthy: Complete Works(Pbk)
The Art of Andy Goldsworthy: Complete Works (Hbk)
Andy Goldsworthy in Close-Up (Pbk)
Andy Goldsworthy in Close-Up (Hbk)
Land Art: A Complete Guide
Richard Long: The Art of Walking
The Art of Richard Long: Complete Works (Pbk)
The Art of Richard Long: Complete Works (Hbk)
Richard Long in Close-Up
Land Art In the UK
Land Art in Close-Up
Installation Art in Close-Up
Minimal Art and Artists In the 1960s and After
Colourfield Painting
Land Art DVD, TV documentary
Andy Goldsworthy DVD, TV documentary
The Erotic Object: Sexuality in Sculpture From Prehistory to the Present Day
Sex in Art: Pornography and Pleasure in Painting and Sculpture
Postwar Art
Sacred Gardens: The Garden in Myth, Religion and Art
Glorification: Religious Abstraction in Renaissance and 20th Century Art
Early Netherlandish Painting
Leonardo da Vinci
Piero della Francesca
Giovanni Bellini
Fra Angelico: Art and Religion in the Renaissance
Mark Rothko: The Art of Transcendence
Frank Stella: American Abstract Artist
Jasper Johns: Painting By Numbers
Brice Marden
Alison Wilding: The Embrace of Sculpture
Vincent van Gogh: Visionary Landscapes
Eric Gill: Nuptials of God
Constantin Brancusi: Sculpting the Essence of Things
Max Beckmann
Egon Schiele: Sex and Death In Purple Stockings
Delizioso Fotografico Fervore: Works In Process 1
Sacro Cuore: Works In Process 2
The Light Eternal: J.M.W. Turner
The Madonna Glorified: Karen Arthurs

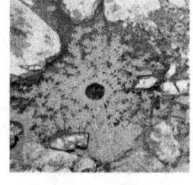

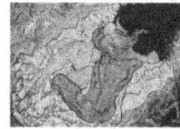

LITERATURE

J.R.R. Tolkien: The Books, The Films, The Whole Cultural Phenomenon
Harry Potter
Sexing Hardy: Thomas Hardy and Feminism
Thomas Hardy's *Tess of the d'Urbervilles*
Thomas Hardy's *Jude the Obscure*
Thomas Hardy: The Tragic Novels
Love and Tragedy: Thomas Hardy
The Poetry of Landscape in Hardy
Wessex Revisited: Thomas Hardy and John Cowper Powys
Wolfgang Iser: Essays
Petrarch, Dante and the Troubadours
Maurice Sendak and the Art of Children's Book Illustration
Andrea Dworkin
Cixous, Irigaray, Kristeva: The *Jouissance* of French Feminism
Julia Kristeva: Art, Love, Melancholy, Philosophy, Semiotics and Psychoanalysis
Hélene Cixous I Love You: The *Jouissance* of Writing
Luce Irigaray: Lips, Kissing, and the Politics of Sexual Difference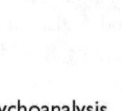
Peter Redgrove: Here Comes the Flood
Peter Redgrove: Sex-Magic-Poetry-Cornwall
Lawrence Durrell: Between Love and Death, East and West
Love, Culture & Poetry: Lawrence Durrell
Cavafy: Anatomy of a Soul
German Romantic Poetry: Goethe, Novalis, Heine, Hölderlin, Schlegel, Schiller
Feminism and Shakespeare
Shakespeare: Selected Sonnets
Shakespeare: Love, Poetry & Magic
The Passion of D.H. Lawrence
D.H. Lawrence: Symbolic Landscapes
D.H. Lawrence: Infinite Sensual Violence
Rimbaud: Arthur Rimbaud and the Magic of Poetry
The Ecstasies of John Cowper Powys
Sensualism and Mythology: The Wessex Novels of John Cowper Powys
Amorous Life: John Cowper Powys and the Manifestation of Affectivity (H.W. Fawkner)
Postmodern Powys: New Essays on John Cowper Powys (Joe Boulter)
Rethinking Powys: Critical Essays on John Cowper Powys
Paul Bowles & Bernardo Bertolucci
Rainer Maria Rilke
In the Dim Void: Samuel Beckett
Samuel Beckett Goes into the Silence
André Gide: Fiction and Fervour
Jackie Collins and the Blockbuster Novel
Blinded By Her Light: The Love-Poetry of Robert Graves
The Passion of Colours: Travels In Mediterranean Lands
Poetic Forms
The Dolphin-Boy

POETRY

The Best of Peter Redgrove's Poetry
Peter Redgrove: Here Comes The Flood
Peter Redgrove: Sex-Magic-Poetry-Cornwall
Ursula Le Guin: Walking In Cornwall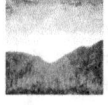
Dante: Selections From the Vita Nuova
Petrarch, Dante and the Troubadours
William Shakespeare: Selected Sonnets
Blinded By Her Light: The Love-Poetry of Robert Graves
Emily Dickinson: Selected Poems
Emily Brontë: Poems
Thomas Hardy: Selected Poems
Percy Bysshe Shelley: Poems
John Keats: Selected Poems
D.H. Lawrence: Selected Poems
Edmund Spenser: Poems
John Donne: Poems
Henry Vaughan: Poems
Sir Thomas Wyatt: Poems
Robert Herrick: Selected Poems
Rilke: Space, Essence and Angels in the Poetry of Rainer Maria Rilke
Rainer Maria Rilke: Selected Poems
Friedrich Hölderlin: Selected Poems
Arseny Tarkovsky: Selected Poems
Arthur Rimbaud: Selected Poems
Arthur Rimbaud: A Season in Hell
Arthur Rimbaud and the Magic of Poetry
D.J. Enright: By-Blows
Jeremy Reed: Brigitte's Blue Heart
Jeremy Reed: Claudia Schiffer's Red Shoes
Gorgeous Little Orpheus
Radiance: New Poems
Crescent Moon Book of Nature Poetry
Crescent Moon Book of Love Poetry
Crescent Moon Book of Mystical Poetry
Crescent Moon Book of Elizabethan Love Poetry
Crescent Moon Book of Metaphysical Poetry
Crescent Moon Book of Romantic Poetry
Pagan America: New American Poetry

MEDIA, CINEMA, FEMINISM and CULTURAL STUDIES

J.R.R. Tolkien: The Books, The Films, The Whole Cultural Phenomenon
Harry Potter
Cixous, Irigaray, Kristeva: The *Jouissance* of French Feminism
Julia Kristeva: Art, Love, Melancholy, Philosophy, Semiotics and   Psychoanalysis
Luce Irigaray: Lips, Kissing, and the Politics of Sexual Difference
Hélène Cixous I Love You: The *Jouissance* of Writing
Andrea Dworkin
'Cosmo Woman': The World of Women's Magazines
Women in Pop Music
Discovering the Goddess (Geoffrey Ashe)
The Poetry of Cinema
The Sacred Cinema of Andrei Tarkovsky (Pbk and Hbk)
Paul Bowles & Bernardo Bertolucci
Media Hell: Radio, TV and the Press
An Open Letter to the BBC
Detonation Britain: Nuclear War in the UK
Feminism and Shakespeare
Wild Zones: Pornography, Art and Feminism
Sex in Art: Pornography and Pleasure in Painting and Sculpture
Sexing Hardy: Thomas Hardy and Feminism

In my view *The Light Eternal* is among the very best of all the material I read on Turner. (Douglas Graham, director of the Turner Museum, Denver, Colorado)

The Light Eternal is a model monograph, an exemplary job. The subject matter of the book is beautifully organised and dead on beam. (Lawrence Durrell)

It is amazing for me to see my work treated with such passion and respect. (Andrea Dworkin)

Sex-Magic-Poetry-Cornwall is a very rich essay... It is like a brightly-lighted box. (Peter Redgrove)

CRESCENT MOON PUBLISHING
P.O. Box 393, Maidstone, Kent, ME14 5XU, United Kingdom.
01622-729593 (UK) 01144-1622-729593 (US) 0044-1622-729593 (other territories)
cresmopub@yahoo.co.uk   www.crescentmoon.org.uk

www.ingramcontent.com/pod-product-compliance
Lightning Source LLC
LaVergne TN
LVHW022111080426
835511LV00007B/759